Whistle for a Possum

(and other Papuan tales)

Translated and Written

by Barbara Lunow

"When small communities abandon their languages...there is a massive disruption in the transfer of traditional knowledge across generations."
Russ Rymer, "Vanishing Voices," National Geographic, July 2012

"One of the acknowledged signs that a people or culture is on the verge of extinction is that knowledge no longer gets transmitted from generation to generation."
Sabine Kuegler, "Child of the Jungle," Page 211

Drawings created by Gersom Saiba, a tribal school boy
Map created by Anna Clover
Photographs by Barbara Lunow

ISBN 13: 978-0692783948
ISBN 10: 0692783946

D W B   P U B L I S H I N G
www.dancingwithbearpublishing.com

Sudohom Areg Eneya Anggÿi Aimugtut.
En moho dag Sogora

Gorsom Saiba.

Drawing created by a 15 year-old Sough school boy

Contents

Map of Papua, Indonesia

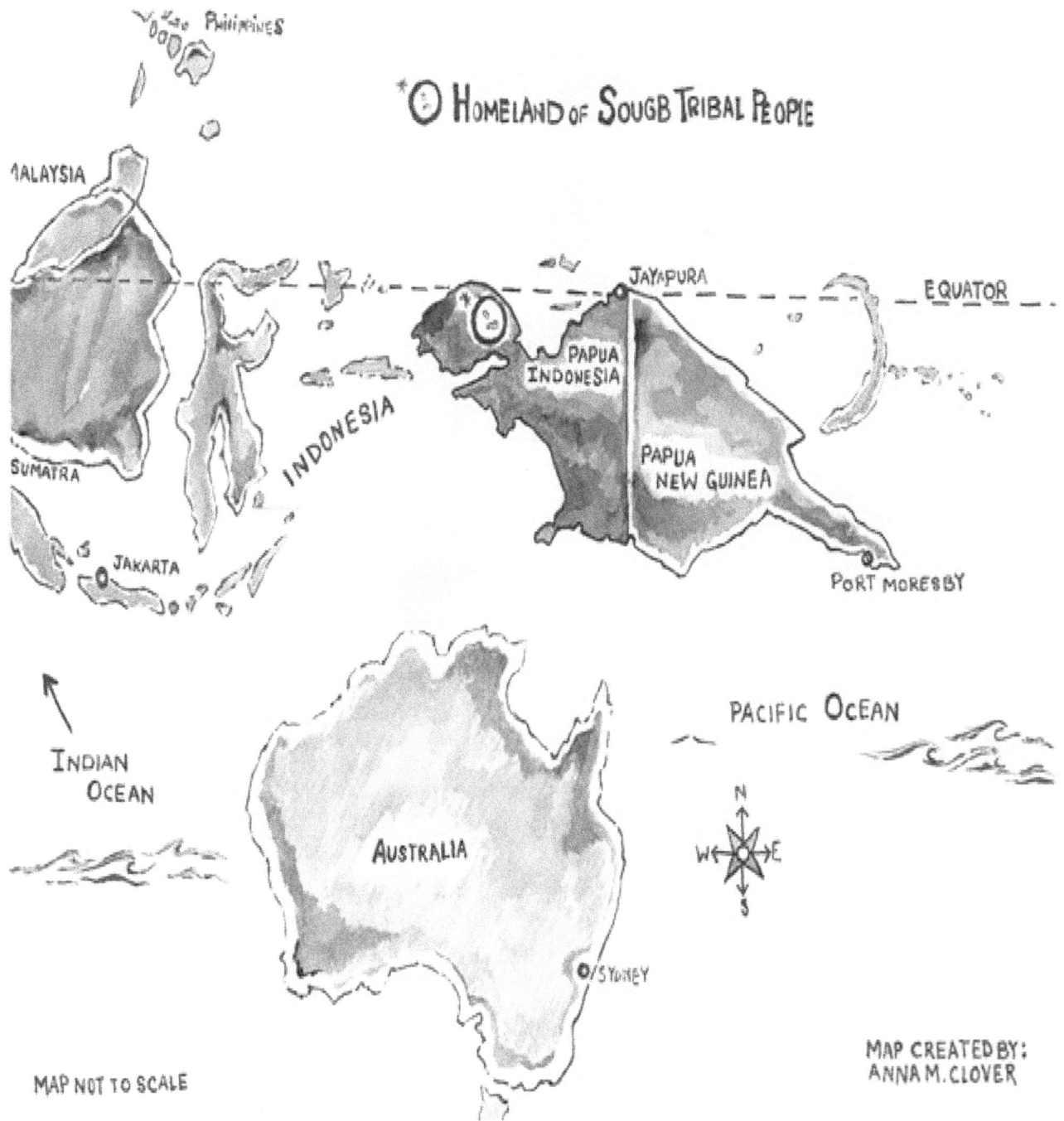

*○ HOMELAND OF SOUGB TRIBAL PEOPLE

Philippines

MALAYSIA

SUMATRA

INDONESIA

JAKARTA

JAYAPURA

EQUATOR

PAPUA INDONESIA

PAPUA NEW GUINEA

PORT MORESBY

INDIAN OCEAN

PACIFIC OCEAN

AUSTRALIA

SYDNEY

N
W   E
S

MAP NOT TO SCALE

MAP CREATED BY:
ANNA M. CLOVER

Author's Notes:

This book contains stories and articles about the primitive Sougb tribe of Papua, Indonesia. They number about 13,000 and live in the far western part of the island of New Guinea. Linguists have identified over 850 distinct language groups and cultures on the island, and the Sougb people comprise one of those groups.

The Sougb language (also listed as Manikion) was spoken orally until it was written down in the 1960s. My husband, Wolfgang (Dan), and I worked and lived among the Sougb people from 1969-2000. The Sougb New Testament was printed in 1996, followed by a shorter Old Testament in 2008, with other church and cultural materials translated in between. After we left Papua, Wolfgang returned every two years for two-three months until 2015. During that time, we continued working on translation projects and he encouraged the Sougb church. Besides the two of us, former missionaries Henry Bock, Patricia Fillmore, and Susan Moers are the only westerners who speak the language and understand the culture.

There are many similar people groups around the world. Because we live in a global community which is growing closer together through advances in communication and ever changing technology, it is important that we preserve the oral histories of these ethnic communities before they are lost and forgotten. We will value and work peaceably with other peoples and nations as we learn more about them and their cultures.

It is my hope and prayer you, the reader, will gain greater understanding and appreciation of one of the many unknown people groups of the world through these translated stories.

Barbara K. Lunow

Fort Mill, SC, May 2016

A Letter

This letter is from me, Dessy Saiba, from the village of Sunggwadis, Papua, Indonesia. Mei-ji-re-so, your life and health to you, my friends in the West.

This book of many stories is about my people, my culture and where I live. Before you read it, I hope you will read this letter, because it explains things that you do not know about us. There are about 13,000 in our tribe. We live in the western half of the island of New Guinea in Papua, Indonesia. New Guinea is the large island north of Australia. The Sougb language is from a branch of the Melanesian languages of the south Pacific islanders. There are over 850 different languages and tribal cultures on this island. We call ourselves the Sougb (So-gb) which means "The People." For many years, outsiders called us the "Manikion Tribe," which means the dredges left over from cooking coconut oil down. We did not appreciate that name.

History of the Sougb Tribe

My ancestors lived in lowland jungles and rain forests of the mountains for hundreds of years, untouched by the outside world. The Sougb and other tribes were separated by natural boundaries such as rivers, valleys and mountains. They were always fighting with each other, using bows, arrows, spears and stone axes. It was necessary to protect their territories from invading enemy groups. The oldest living ones in my tribe (we call them the Grandfathers), tell stories of head-hunting and eating their enemies in the wars before my time. Other tribes are still hostile to outsiders and continue fighting with each other. We Sougb now live peaceably with neighboring tribes and among ourselves.

Generations ago, foreigners with yellow and white skins came to our island in sailing ships to explore and take slaves. They called the Papuan natives "Stone Age People," because they only used stone axes. The Sougb were one of the early groups who traded with the sailors for steel axes and machetes (long, wide-bladed knives). They traded brilliantly colored Birds-of-Paradise feathers, camphor wood and cinnamon bark for tools, axes, knives, glass-beads and dowry cloth that the foreigners brought by boat. When my people saw that the people on the ships were also hunting slaves, some of them moved farther into the jungle and many more went into the mountains to hide.

In my grandfathers' time, years after the trading ships came, Dutch soldiers walked through Sougb lands. They set up a government post across the lake from where I live. We were under Dutch rule for many years. Now we are ruled by the government of Indonesia. It was the Dutch soldiers who went on patrols in the jungle and the mountains and made us stop fighting other tribes. Once in a while, the soldiers led medical teams into our land. They treated my people for bad sores, coughs, malaria and other infections—whatever they saw that day.

The Dutch opened schools in the Malay language. At first only boys were allowed to attend. Village elders said that girls needed to work in the gardens and help their mothers watch the younger children. At that time, the men believed girls didn't have the brains to learn anything. It was like this for many years until the fathers and uncles finally permitted a few of their girls to be educated in the mid 1980's. Since then, many girls have gone to school and learned to be teachers, nurses and government clerks.

After the schools opened, we were no longer isolated from other cultures. When the teenage boys finished elementary school in the village, they traveled to two coastal towns for middle school and high school. Leaving our tribal customs and quiet villages behind, they entered into the coastal towns: bright lights in the stores, night life in the markets, and the traffic with cars. When the students came back to the village, they were proud to speak Indonesian and talk about things they did in town. The women and children couldn't understand them because they didn't want to speak in the Sougb language any more. Not only that, but when we gathered around our home fires at night they shamed their elders, saying it was boring to listen to their old stories of past history. The young men also didn't want to obey and follow our tribal traditions and rules any longer.

About this Book

      This book tells about the Sougb tribe with cultural stories, folktales, and fun language exercises. The stories were passed down from generation to generation as the old people recited them from memory around the fires in our bark houses. All of our tales were told over and over until we remembered them by heart. It was this way, because no words of our language were written down at that time. It was good when the missionaries came, because they wrote our words on paper and taught us how to read. The adults were greatly pleased because they never went to government schools. They learned to read in the literacy classes that the missionaries taught. Many children also learned to read the Sougb language before going to government schools, and when they entered public school, they learned to read Indonesian very quickly.

      When Mama Lunow saw the young people going away to school and no longer treasuring our Sougb language and history, her heart was sad. She was afraid that if the old stories were not passed down to the younger generation, the history of the Sougb would soon be lost and forgotten. We worked together to write the stories on paper. At first I told her things my grandmother and my father told me before they died. Then we walked around the lake to villages and asked the old people to share their words and memories in the Sougb voice with us.

      All of those stories are already printed in the Sougb Culture Reader. My heart tells me that it is good to have this book, because many of the Old Ones who told the stories have died. With the culture book printed, we will always remember the old ones and their stories.

      Listen to my voice, because at first only a few of the adults wanted to read the stories. But now the young people are reading and sharing the book with friends from other tribes. They too, want to hear the stories because their tribal stories are similar to ours. The young people are finally realizing that their tribal history and culture are important, especially for future generations. We also have other books in our language, including the Bible. When we see these books in print, we know that Sougb is a real language that will never die out. The shame in our tribal voice has turned to pride.

Since the foreigners and missionaries came into our land, life has changed in many ways. Our eyes and minds are opening to new ideas and knowledge. We have gone to the cities and learned more about a world of other cultures and languages, of cell phones, television, computers, and technology. Many of the Sougb people have moved to the coast to live near the towns. But a great number of my people still live in the interior, in the jungles and mountains. We women plant our sweet potato gardens like we have always done. However, the plowed road and four-wheel drive cars coming through our land remind us that we live in a larger world than our own.

All of my words to you are true and right. I heard these stories with my own ears. And I saw some of these things with my own eyes.

Meijireso, your life to you, my friends in the West,

From me, Dessy, your friend from the Sougb tribe

Children's Stories & Instructions

1. When I was a little girl, my grandmother told me stories about animals and birds that talked and did things like people. She repeated the stories to me like they were true. I do not know if this story is real, or not. It was written on paper by a young boy when the Sougb people were first learning to read and write. In the story, Raven's name, Aig-ba, is also one of the family clan names in my tribe. —Dessy

Father Raven Adopts Baby Cockatoo
A Sougb Folktale

Cockatoo Birds

Father Raven, who was also named *Aigba,* was walking along the beach.
There he found a baby cockatoo sitting alone on the sand.

He carried the baby bird home to his house.

Raven protected and fed Baby Cockatoo until he got bigger.

One day, he made a bow and arrows and gave them to Young Cockatoo.

He taught him how to hunt and shoot with his bow and arrows.

The next day Cockatoo went hunting by himself, and he shot a bird and a possum.

He brought both of them home for Father Aigba.

Raven gratefully ate the gifts from his adopted son Young Cockatoo.

Think about the story: Cockatoo honored his adoptive Father by giving his first catch to him.

1. In what ways might you show honor and respect to someone who has raised you and taught you how to live and behave?
2. Think of other examples of someone taking care of another person who is not a family member?

2. *Sougb boys like hunting with their bows and arrows. They hunt for birds, furry tree possums and rats. When hunting for large jungle rats, they make traps in the tall grasses, stand still and wait. When the rat sticks its nose in the grass noose, they shoot it with an arrow. They build a fire out in the jungle and eat their catch before going home. Boys still hunt with bows and arrows today. Samen was a young boy in a literacy class learning how to read and write when he wrote this story. —Dessy*

Whistle for a Possum
Schoolboy Samen Saiba, Literacy Class 1964

Pet Possum (Tree Kangaroo)

When I hunt, I use my bow and arrows.

Hunting in the mountains, I search for signs of possum.

If I see a possum up in a tree, I whistle, and it will sit still and listen.

Then I take aim and shoot, and put it in my string bag.

Later, I will roast it over my fire.

I also like to hunt birds.

First, I quietly hide myself and watch.

If a bird flies up out of a tree, or swoops down to the ground,

I can shoot it and put it in my little string bag also.

One bird is not enough, so I keep hiding out of sight.

If I don't hide, the bird might see me, or hear me, and fly away.

Even if it takes a long time, I stay quiet and wait for another bird to come near.

When I hunt, I use my bow and arrows.

Think about this:

1. What is the boy's secret strategy for catching a possum?
2. What are his main tactics for hunting birds?
3. Why do you think the boy wanted to catch more than one bird?
4. Do you think there is a difference between hunting for sport and hunting to eat? If so, explain.

3. *Yunus Saiba grew up in a mountain village. He never learned to read and write, but he passed down the tribal myths and folktales to his children, the same way his father told them to him. The children especially liked stories about animals that talked and acted human. —Dessy*

Smaiy and Wuneejo Have a Bad Day
Yunus Saiba, Sunggwadis Village

Young boys hunting

Two dogs, Smaiy and Wuneejo, were tracking a possum by following his scent on the trail.

Suddenly they both stopped and pointed their noses in the air.

And there he was, clever Mr. Possum was sitting in a tall tree, high up on a branch.

He was not fooled at all by their whistles for him.

Possum looked down with a sneer, mocking the two hunting dogs below him,

> "Hey, Smaiy! Hey, Wuneejo!
>
> Heh, heh, Smaiy! Heh, heh, Wuneejo!
>
> What's the matter? Huh?
>
> Did you catch anything? Have you bitten, tasted, anything yet?
>
> What about eating something? Come on, tell me, did you eat yet?"
>
> After Mr. Possum teased them, he scurried higher up the branches.

He ran farther away from the dogs, nimbly jumping through the air to a nearby tree.

Totally out of reach for Smaiy and Wuneejo, he stopped and rested there.

Mr. Possum turned his head and looked back at the two hunting dogs with a sneer.

Then he grinned and gave one great laugh, loud and long, and he speedily jumped from tree top to tree top, right out of their sight.

What about this story:

1. What makes this a funny story?
2. What do you think Smaiy and Wuneejo had to eat that night?
3. In what ways are other forest animals clever in not being caught?

4. *When I was a little girl, I wanted to hear all the old folktales and stories. The oldest son usually hid these stories in his heart and repeated them to his brothers and sisters. But I asked my father to tell them to me so that I could pass them on to my children. The story below is one that my father told me, like it really happened. It is about a grasshopper and a rat, and I don't think that either one of them was a true friend. —Dessy*

Rat and Grasshopper and the Banana Tree
Desijohota Saiba, Sunggwadis Village

Children with jungle rats

Once there was a man who had a banana tree. He took care of his tree, watering it day and night, all the time. The man watched over his tree, waiting for the young bananas to grow on the stalk and ripen.

One day when the bananas were nearly ripe, Amosda (a grasshopper), and his friend Eejoh (a jungle rat), also saw the ripe fruit on the tree. "Hey, Eejoh, look, the bananas on that tree are ripe. Why don't you go climb up the banana tree? Climb up the tree and get some bananas for us."

But Eejoh answered back to his friend, "Uh-uh, not me, Amosda, you do it. You go on, go ahead and climb the tree for us."

"Nah, Eejoh, you climb up!"

"Oh no, not me, Amosda. You do it yourself, go climb up there!"

And so it went, back and forth between the two friends. They kept at each other, but neither one wanted to climb the banana tree.

Finally, the next day when the bananas were soft and yellow, Eejoh decided he would climb the banana tree after all. But Amosda only sat in the shade under the tree and waited.

Looking up the trunk of the tree, he called "See, way up there on top? That's my hand of bananas."

Eejoh paid no attention to him. He picked a banana and sat eating it himself. Then he threw the peeling down on Amosda at the bottom of the tree.

Amosda yelled, "Hey, what is this banana skin for? Why did you throw it at me?"

But Eejoh didn't answer a word. He kept eating bananas and throwing the peelings down to the ground. After he was full, Eejoh hurried back down the banana tree, but he didn't bring even one banana down for his friend.

The grasshopper couldn't believe it. By then his *heart was hot* against Rat, and he hit him hard. The blow knocked Eejoh down. The punch surprised him and he was so scared that he ran into the jungle and hid. Amosda followed and tried to find him, but he didn't see him hiding in the thick bushes and grasses. Amosda turned around and stomped home. His heart remained hot towards his friend.

Later, in the afternoon when Amosda was sitting at home, Grandmother Grasshopper asked, "Why aren't you out playing with your friend, Eejoh? I haven't seen him all day."

But the grasshopper only partly answered his grandmother, telling her in a grumpy voice, "Oh, he's around here somewhere. He himself knows where he's at. I don't keep track of him and know where he is all the time."

Think about this story:

Neither one of the friends would forgive the other. They no longer spoke to each other.

1. What do you think happened next to the two friends?
2. What would they have to do before they could make up?
3. How would you respond if you were Grasshopper? Friend Rat?
4. Think about the man who planted the banana tree. How do you think he felt when he found his bananas missing?

5. *Many generations ago, in my grandfathers' time, we Sougb did not have a written language. When the whiteskins came to study our voice, they wrote it down for us. Our words sound different from any other language in the world. Would you like to learn some fun and funny words from the Sougb language? —Dessy*

Sneezes, Belches and Hiccups
(Imitating Words-Onomatopoeia)

What do these words have in common?

biff	boom	bang	snap	crackle
pop	wheeze	whoosh	whiz	bop

They are all *onomatopoeia* (an-a-mat'-to-pe'-a), words that are formed by imitating their sounds. Our English language has many such words. Can you think of any other words that sound like these words? What did you come up with? How about *ah-choo?* Or *chirp* and *cheep? Hiss? Buzz?*

Other cultures around the world also have onomatopoeia in their languages and each language expresses them differently. The Sougb people of Papua, Indonesia are a tribal group of 13,000. They live in the jungles and mountainous rain forests. The Sougb language also has unique imitating words. They are fun words to say and learn.

Here's a word-challenge game:
See if you can match up the English word with the Sougb word.

sneeze	e-ji-sa
belch	een-yoom-da
pass gas	e-chee
shake, shiver	e-ching-ga
hiccup	booch
earthquake rumble	chin-cho-ko-bed

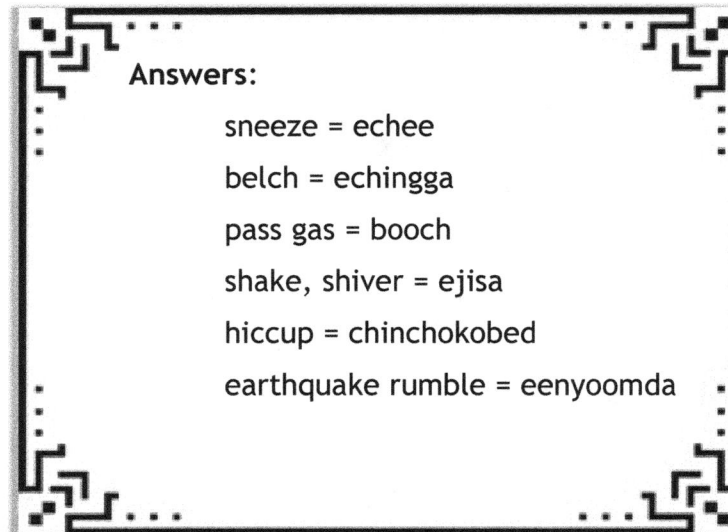

Answers:

      sneeze = echee

      belch = echingga

      pass gas = booch

      shake, shiver = ejisa

      hiccup = chinchokobed

      earthquake rumble = eenyoomda

6. *My people lived in isolation for hundreds of years in territory un-mapped by the western world. The Sougb only had machetes, axes and cooking pots. Modern technology was completely unknown to us. In my lifetime, our language was put into writing with the translator using just a typewriter at first, and then we were introduced to computers. Other modern day tools and instruments have also come into our culture: mobile phones, satellite TVs, watches and clocks. The wrist watch is a coveted item for all of us. These things have brought the schedule of daily life from the outside world into our normal patterns of village living. Even though many Sougb proudly wear wrist watches, they still look at the clock in the sky to tell time. —Dessy*

What Time Is It?

(The Sougb Clock)

Petu Saiba, Sururay Village

4 AM	"heaven (sky) shows a fine line of darkness and light," *bo-go er-ech-i-ra-ha*
5 AM	"heavens break up," *bo-go o-bru-rugb*
6 AM	"light of day, it comes, it comes," *lo-na-men-men*
7 AM	"sun throws out his feet," *ig-da er-ba mo-ho-ra*
8-10 AM	"sun brings/gives heat," *ig-des o-hu des-logb*
11-12 Noon	"sun touches the heavens," *ig-da-bo-go*
1-2 PM	"sun turns his body sideways," *ig-da eh-in ma-ga*
3-4 PM	"sun bends over," *ig-da e-day-j*
5-6 PM	"sun falls behind the horizon," *lo-sog*
6-7 PM	"sun fell already," *ig-da ob-sa-re-so-hob*
	"light and the darkness meet together," *lo-mooch-mooch*

12 MN   "moon closes over the sky bringing the darkness,"

lo-bay-ng-mod

Let's learn how to tell time in the Sougb language:

1. Look carefully at each Sougb word and figure out the meanings of words that are repeated, like: igda, bogo?

2. If you didn't have a clock, how would you describe the time from the sun: Morning?   Noon?   Afternoon?   Evening?

3. What is your favorite description in telling time by the sun and why?

7. *How many times has your mom or your teacher told you not to count with your fingers? Do you do it in your head when you are trying to figure out a math problem, or sneak your hands under your desk to count your fingers as you look innocently at your teacher? The Sougb people also have a "hands on" system for counting, which they've used for generations. And it's okay with their moms too. —Barbara Lunow*

One Finger, Two Toes
(Counting System)

Look below and try to follow the instructions after each number as you learn to count in the Sougb language.

Number:			Motion, description
One	(1)	=	*hom* ...right hand grasps the left thumb
Two	(2)	=	*hwai* ...right hand grasps thumb and forefinger
Three	(3)	=	*ho-moy* ...right hand " " " two fingers
Four	(4)	=	*ho-gu* ... " " " " " three fingers
Five	(5)	=	*ser-gem* ... " " " all left hand fingers, or one hand in a fist
Six	(6)	=	*seng-gem* ...left hand grasps the right thumb
Seven	(7)	=	*seng-gai* ... left hand " " " " and forefinger
Eight	(8)	=	*seng-ge-moi* .. " " " " " " two fingers
Nine	(9)	=	*seng-ge-gu* ... " " " " " " three fingers
Ten	(10)	=	*si-sa* two hand hands, with palms together, "*mesira hwai*," two hands
Fifteen	(15)	=	*so-ra-ma* two hands, plus grasp one foot, Or "*me-si-ra hwai, mo-ho-ra hom*," two hands, one foot
Twenty	(20)	=	*sud hom* (one person) two hands and two feet Or "*me-si-ra hwai, mo-ho-ra hwai*"
Thirty	(30)	=	*sud hom sisa e-de-su* one person, plus two hands "*sud hom; dara mai-re-si, da-ra me-bes, da-ra mums, da-ra mops, da-ra marij*" One person: plus eyes, ears, nose holes, lips and breasts

Forty   (40) =   *sud hwai*   two people

Fifty   (50)   =   *sud hwai sisa e-desu*   two people, plus two hands

Sixty   (60)   =   *sud ho-moy*   three people

One hundred   =   *sud ser-gem*   five people

Great Many   =   "B*an au-gwan, dan au-gwan,*"

                              All of you, all of me, more than anyone can count

Try counting the Sougb way:

1. Count by fives using your fingers, hands, feet and toes: 5, 10, 15, 20

2. Which number is the hardest for you to perform?

3. Show us your age by using your hands and feet.

4. Ask an adult their age and then show it by using other people.

*8. My grandfathers, In-dou and Snaugb-men, told me many things when I was a little girl. My father, Si-je-ray, repeated these same rules over and over to my sisters, brothers, and me when we sat close to his fire at night in our bark house. His voice spoke to us, saying, "If you follow these rules, you will have **lusud mos**, mature adult skin. If you behave this way, you will have a good reputation and people will respect you. They will trust you and not be afraid to visit in your house." All my life, I remembered what my father and grandfathers told me and I tried to follow everything they taught me. —Grandmother Dogor*

Following Your Father's Voice
Dogor Saiba, Sururay Village

Guard your eyes, and your hands, and your feet, and also your ears and your tongue, and your whole body.

1. **Your eyes:** Guard your eyes. When you look, you think on it in your head, then it enters your heart. Your hands reach out to touch it, while b*an ab-doch e-trij i-chi-ra,* your heart flutters over it and you will keep wishing for it and finally take it.

   This also means *ban be-se-dou-gwo ban ab-i-re-si, you guard your eyes* from continually looking at a girl or boy. When you watch them, your heart flutters after them, too.

2. **Your hands:** Guard your hands from stealing. Don't take anything from others— not their corn, or squash, or any other food from their gardens. Do not take their firewood, machetes, and never take their pigs. I tell you not to take one thing that is not your own.

This also means *ban be-se-dou-gwo ban ab-si-ra, keep your hands off* other girls or boys, because if you touch them *ban ab-doch an len, your heart will lean towards* them too.

3. **Your feet**: Keep your feet from just wandering. Don't go up into anyone else's house where you do not belong and where you will learn other things than what your father tells you.

   Follow your father's warning and don't go to dances. If you do, you will see other girls or boys and you will like each other. B*an be-me-dreg ban a-bi-na men ge-se-dou-gwo da-ra en mer* means, do not step outside of your father's care and advice.

4. **Your ears and tongue**: Guard your ears and tongue from listening and talking about other people's affairs. Close your ears to their business and do not talk about it.

   This means *ban bo-wun ban ab-doch mes, be-se-dou-gwo ban ab-te-mou-wu, lower your heart and keep your tongue* from telling what you know about other people to someone else. If you gossip about others, in a little while it will grow into a big affair.

5. **Your body**: Guard your body from doing what is wrong, the things your father has warned you about. Don't go down the path that is bad and wicked, following your own way. Instead, follow the instructions and warnings of your father and grandfathers.

   This also means *ban be-se-dou-gwo ban a-ba-ga, always keep your body* from other girls or boys, because your father will help you to choose a husband or wife.

Consider the rules of conduct for the Sougb children:

1. How would you reword the rules for children today?

   Your eyes?

   Your hands?

   Your feet?

   Your ears and tongue?

   Your whole body?

2. What do we have in our culture/belief system today like these rules and instructions?

*9. In my earliest years, my mother whispered a little rhyme in my ear, over and over again. I remember it still. The poem told me '**be-sa-ra bo-hwa-ra**', to work diligently and be generous. This was my duty as a girl in my culture. My people had certain rules of conduct for boys and girls that our fathers and mothers taught us. We were to follow these instructions all our lives. We listed some of the teachings of the grandfathers in an early writing class. —Dessy*

Dos and Don'ts
(Laws of the Grandfathers)

1. Grown-ups awaken their children in the morning, saying: Don't sleep until full daylight. Get up and listen to the voices of the adults in your house. Let your hearts trust in their words always. When you get children of your own, teach them the same rules so their hearts will trust in what you teach them. This is what will make you wise in your life.

2. Grandfathers warned their children like this: Don't sleep so deeply that you can't get up to attend to your duties in the morning. Be ready and diligent to search for your own wealth and riches. You cannot do this if you sleep in.

3. Grown-ups teach their children to honor them, like this: Don't go about on your own, following other children and what they do. If you go out on your own, we do not know what you are doing. But if you always *os ma-ga*, hang on to my body, which means to take our advice and follow our voice, then we can stand by your name. Your reputation will hold true.

4. Grown-ups tell their children how to show respect to others, saying: Do good things for your aunts and other relatives. Then they will help you with what you need when you have *lu-sud mos*, mature skin, are an adult.

5. Grown-ups warn their children about how they should talk, saying: Don't speak in a nasty way to your elders. If your speech is like that, they will be afraid of you and stay away from you. They will not want to help you, either.

6. Finally, adults warn the children about what is not safe or good for them, saying like this:

> Don't touch the fire, it burns.
>
> Be careful of eating this plant—it will make you sick.
>
> Be careful of following what others do—you could lose your reputation.
>
> Beware of going near the lakeshore where the *Anes,* a spirit, lives. He will capture you.

Think about this:

1. Why do Sougb parents warn against sleeping in?
2. Why do you have to get up in the morning?
3. Which Sougb rules are similar to the ones you learned?
4. Which rules do you think are most important to follow?
5. Compare these rules to rules you have been taught. How are they alike? Different?

History of the Sougb People

Old woman with untrimmed hair

10. *This is a true story about the first Sougb man to see the two lakes where many Sougb people now live. His footprints are the first ones beside the lakes. This story was also passed down by word of mouth, but now we have it in writing and printed in a book. —Dessy*

Buchgemehir Leaves His Footprints
Grandfather Yonaden Ahoren, Kofo Village

Mountain village in rain forest

A long time ago a man named Buch-ge-me-hir and his wife came from the coastal town of Moosdir (also called Ransiki). They climbed up the mountains from the seashore until they arrived near the Girl Lake, which we call *Ang-gi Gi-da.*

The waters were blue and clear, and so they stopped to hunt eel. They damned up the water along the shore so they could catch them in shallow waters. The lake was full of eel, and they caught more than they could eat. They built a rack of sticks tied with vines to dry the eels in the sun. Then they made a fire using green wood underneath to smoke them.

"I am going up the mountain to see the other side," Buchgemehir told his wife, "Don't eat the eels' stomachs while I am gone."

He left his wife and climbed the mountain so he could get a good look at the other lake. But there were too many trees surrounding that lake. He couldn't see *Anggi Giji*, Boy Lake, very well. As he stared at the water through the forest, black clouds formed in the sky and dropped down over the lake and mountain tops. He thought this was a bad sign, telling him that maybe his wife had *gone beyond his voice,* disobeyed, and had eaten the eels' insides that he had warned her about. He turned around and hurried down the mountain. When he got back to Anggi Gida it was too late. His wife lay there dead. She had not listened to his voice, his warnings.

Buchgemehir's *me-doch mo-mo-go*, his heart was truly sad about his wife's death, and he decided not to go over the mountain and down to the shores of Anggi Giji, the other lake. He only wanted to sit there and mourn for his wife. After many days of crying, he finally got up one morning and walked back down through the rain forest to his home at the seashore.

This is why we say Buchgemehir *left his footprints* by the lakes, because he was the first one to see them, but he never lived there.

Stop and consider this story:

1. What do you think *"he left his footprints by the lake"* means?
2. How would you like to leave your footprints on this earth?
3. What are your dreams for your life?

11. *Names are important to the Sougb people. They all have meanings: when an event happened, or where a person came from, or some other distinct shape of an object. This is how we remember names and people together. Grandfather Yonaden is one of the elders of the Ahoren clan and he knows many of their stories. This is the Ahoren story about how the lakes were named. –Dessy*

Boy Lake-Girl Lake

Grandfather Yonaden Ahoren, Kofo Village

Cloud cover over Boy Lake

When my Grandfather Ahoren first entered this land he thought the lakes should be named after a place called *Makasa*, the land where the foreigners came from long ago. So he named the lakes located here *Anggi Giji*, Boy Lake, and *Anggi*

Gida, Girl Lake. He named them that because he thought they were like a man and a woman, like the people who came from the far away land of Makasa.

The meaning of the names for the lakes:

1. **Anggi Giji** stands for *mok-mok,* bad or evil, fearsome, showing power and strength like the men of the Sougb tribe. The Boy Lake also looks like the *ansee,* which are the dark, stagnant pools found on the mountain tops. We are very afraid of them and walk around them so that we avoid touching their waters as much as we can. The spirits in the ansee are the same ones that are in Anggi Giji. We know that because the mountain ponds are black and dark, and spirits hide in them, too.

2. **Anggi Gida** stands for *beautiful water* because the lake looks clean, and pure, and the color of the ocean with sand on the shore. Our women are also more like this lake, mild in manners, beautiful bodies and following our culture and customs. So my grandfather called that lake Girl Lake, or Female Lake. That is how my grandfather named the lakes so long ago.

Consider this:
1. What do you think of the names the Sougb chose for their lakes?

2. Why do you think they chose these names?

3. What names would you give to the lakes?

12. *The ancestors were afraid of lakes, ponds and waterfalls, because they thought dangerous creatures and evil spirits lived in them. Each of the clans have their own stories to tell about the beings they have seen in the deep water places. They were so fearful of the water that no one ever learned how to swim. —Dessy*

Living by the Lake
Grandfather Yonaden Ahoren, Kofo Village

Angii village by Boy Lake

Long ago the Ahoren Grandfathers were terrified of Anggi Lake, its dense woods surrounding the lake shores and the spirits in the dark waters. They never approached it, until one day when my great-Grandfather Ahoren ordered three of his sons to go to the forests by the lake and try to appease the spirits there. When the Ahoren boys walked down through the trees and saw the land, they thought the land

41

around the lake was all good. They went back and reported to their father that they could move closer and make big gardens by the lake shore.

But everyone was still afraid of the *Anes*. This was a spirit with a physical body that lived in Boy Lake. So our grandfather told his sons what to do, "You take the ash from our fire and put it in your bamboo carrying tube. Then go gather the special leaves of our secret flowers, collect the shavings from our secret wood, crush and pound them together to mix with the ashes in the bamboo. Hide the tube away in your net bag and take it down to the lake. Then throw all the powder from the bamboo into the waters of Boy Lake. This is the only way we can keep the Anes from hurting us."

The sons obeyed their father's voice. When they stood at the shores of Lake Anggi Giji, they threw their magic powder into the wind and over the water. This was their gift for Anes, the spirit who slept in the lake. The powdered mixture was to make the Anes feel weak. If his body was weak, surely he couldn't harm them. Once they threw the ashes in the lake, the three sons hurried home to their father.

After many months, our grandfather and his three sons walked down from the mountain ridges to see if Anggi Giji was finally safe enough to live near it. They decided to cut down trees and clear the land for gardens. They built their houses on a plain that was closer to the lake. The sons from the Ahoren family were the first ones to move closer and live beside the lake.

Think about this:

1. Why did Grandfather Ahoren send his sons to the lake?

2. How do you think they all felt when they went down to the lake?

3. What did the sons do so that the Anes would not harm them?

4. How did the Sougb overcome their fears?

5. If you grew up in the Sougb tribe how would you feel living by the lake?

13. *Grandfather Kubei was the oldest man in my village. He was so old that his skin was wrinkled and dry, and his legs were bent because he wasn't able to walk any more. He knew many stories from the Saiba clan. When we asked him about the ancestors, he laughed and was excited to talk about what he remembered from the old days. —Dessy*

Sogora Finds a Wife
Grandfather Kubei, Sunggwadis Village

Our Grandfather So-go-ra came from Man-den and slept at a place called Sa-tob-mod. One day his relatives called him to come to In-yu-hu-may. So he walked across the mountains of Sin-sin-e-mes and U-gwa-mong-ga-mod.

When he arrived at Inyuhumay, his relatives didn't know him and they questioned him, saying: "Where are you from? From the Im-chin? From the I-jom? "

Sogora assured them, "I am from the Ijom."

But the men did not trust him and they challenged him, saying, "If you really are from the Ijom family, then go fight and kill someone from our enemy, the Lou-wi people."

Sogora went out like they told him and fought with the Louwi.

After a while he returned to Inyuhumay for a big dance they were having. Many people climbed up the pole steps to the dance house. Everyone was staring at Sogora again, because he was a stranger to them and, at that time, he had long hair. One girl, Day-a-gar-is, really liked him, especially with his braided hair. But this girl had skin ringworm all over her body. No man wanted her for a wife because her skin was chalky and dry.

During the evening, Sogora stood up before the dance crowd. Chanting and swaying, he sang a song like this:

> *The Louhwi people-o...*
> *The Ha-may-people-o...*
> *They are all dead-o...*

43

See them all dead-o...

The Louhwi-o...

The Hamay-o...

They are all gone-o...

None of them are here-o.

He sang and everyone kept dancing, dancing, *de-de-de-da, de-de-de-da,* just like that.

Then the men from Inyuhumei gathered together and began to sing and chant a new song, singing like this:

Oh, indeed, amazing-o.

What do we have to give to this brave man-o?

We could give him amplog beads-o...

But he doesn't want them, oh, no.

We could give him ampoun beads-o...

But he doesn't want them, no.

We could give him a long knife-o...

But he doesn't want one-o.

All he really wants is that girl-o...

Only her, the one with ringworm-o.

Yes, he really wants that one...

He truly wants her, yo.

The village men went to Sogora and asked him, "Is it true that the only thing you want in payment from us is the one with ringworm all over her skin? The one that no one else will touch?"

Sogora was happy. He chanted back to them, singing another new song, like this:

Yes, her, the one with white skin-o...

Yes, she is really all that I want-o.

She will be my own tree bark...

The one I want to be my own wife.

All other wives have real skin-o...

They all look the same-o.

But my wife, see her skin...

Her white ringworm skin.

No one will touch her-o...

No other man will dare to touch her-o.

So they gave the woman Dayagaris to Sogora to be his wife. They went to live at Satobmod, where she gave birth to their children. These are the first ones of our ancestors from the Saiba clan.

Think about this:

1. Why did Sogora have to fight the Louwi people?

2. What was unusual about the woman, Dayagaris?

3. Why did Sogora want her as his wife?

4. What do you think about his choice?

14. *Old Grandfather sat by his fire talking and laughing, telling us stories from the Saiba clan. His father passed them down to him when he was a young boy sitting around the fire at night. They were the tales of our earliest grandfather, Sogora, when he first came to Anggi Lake. I listened well with my ears, because I had never heard these stories before. —Dessy*

The Saiba's Walk of Discovery
Grandfather Kubei Saiba, Sunggwadis Village

So-go-ro and his wife, Day-a-ga-ris, had two sons named Sno-moch and Ba-ray-mer. Remember, Dayagaris is the wife with white skin, the one with ringworm all over her body. When the boys grew up, Sogora and his sons trekked up the mountains to see what might be up there. They walked through the damp rain forest with so many tall trees they could not see the sun. On the mountain top, they saw only a glimpse of the dark waters of Anggi Lake way down the mountain. They searched and found their way down the other side of the mountain to an area just above a place later named Su-ru-ray. There was more forest below them, and they knew that the great sea of water was not far from there.

They built a *tu meij*, little hut, and the three men began to chop down the *mo-lay-ch* trees in order to clear the land for a garden: for corn, squash, sweet potatoes, and tobacco. After preparing the garden, they returned over the mountain to their home in Sa-tob-mod. In several more months, they came back and everything in the garden was growing, and it all looked good, really and truly it did.

So Sogora talked to Snomoch and Baraymer, instructing them, "You two start to cut down more trees and prepare for a bigger garden. I will go and get the other relatives to come and work with us. While I'm gone, you stay here and cut the *saugwa*, the *steiga*, the *gowi*, the *sirga*, and the *snago* trees, yes, all of them. Get the land ready for a huge family garden.

I'm going back to get everyone now. When we return, we will travel around the mountain ridges on the far side of the dark waters of the lake. Look for the smoke of our fire, coming from way up there near the top. Then you will know it is us and we are coming back."

In a while, Sogora brought all the other relatives to settle in the forest, which was not far above the lake.

Consider the story:

1. What was it about the Anggi Lakes area that scared the Grandfathers of the Sougb?

2. What is the first thing they did to settle by Anggi Lake?

3. When Sogora said he was coming back, what sign did they use to tell him?

4. How would they know when they were close?

15. *Sogora and his family lived over the mountain to the south of Anggi for a long time. But after they saw Anggi Lake and planted a garden there, Sogora wanted his family to live in that new land. Many years ago he brought them all to live here, on my side of the lake. —Dessy*

Sogora Moves His Family to Anggi
Grandfather Kubei Saiba, Sunggwadis Village

In the early days, all of the trees we needed for building our houses grew in the rain forests surrounding the shores of Lake Ang-gi Giji, Boy Lake. The forest was so thick our ancestors could only glimpse the sparkle of water through the trees. When we came, we all freely chopped down trees with thick bark for house flooring. We cut up hardwood trees for bark siding, and we used the thick trunks for foundation poles and the smaller branches for support poles. The special prickly palms stood in clusters on the mountainside and the palm fronds were good for roofing. We took vines from the trees and tied everything together. Later on, we found the balsawood barrel trees and used them to make rafts for going on the lake.

But when everyone first came over the mountains, Grandfather So-go-ro ordered the relatives to help Sno-moch and Ba-ray-mer cut down trees and burn the underbrush from the land around the area of Sururay. As they cut down trees and burned off the brush for gardens and a village, the lake was gradually revealed. But everyone remained afraid of the spirits in the water and they stayed away from the lake shore.

But listen well to my voice—over the mountain on Lake Anggi Gida the water looked like the sea, and there was white sand on the shore. I think maybe *possum hauled sand at night, so the daylight wouldn't come.* At least that is what we say, but we don't really know this for sure. We tell our children that, because the other lake is so beautiful and we don't know why.

After some time, Sogora wanted to explore and so he went through the forest around the lake to a place called Kor-pray-mod. When he looked there, he knew it was a better place to live. But then he stopped and thought to himself, "Anggi Giji is like a deep, dark, scary waterhole. We dare not build our houses here yet, because it is so close to the lake."

It was many years before the Saiba clan moved farther down the mountains towards the lake. They chopped down many trees and planted many gardens, before the lake became visible.

Consider how the Saiba clan moved to Anggi Lake:

1. The Saibas used all natural material from the forests and jungle for their houses. Give some examples of what they used.
2. What did they see as they cleared the land for gardens?
3. When did they start moving down the mountain and closer to the lake?
4. Why do you think they wanted to move closer to the lake?

16. *The In-yo-mu-s clan lives across the lake now, but they came from over the mountains near us long ago. This is their story, from an old man who was nearly blind in his eyes but he could see very well in his thoughts. —Dessy*

Inyomus Comes to Anggi
Grandfather Ijom-medigo, Disihu Village

Warrior dressed for battle

One day a long time ago, when they were not at war between tribes, In-yo-mus and I-hweij came from Di-rir-bo Mountain to get orchid fibers to make their woven hip-bands, G-strings. When they climbed up to the top of U-gwa-mong-ga-mod Mountain, they spied Lake Anggi Giji. But when they saw the lake they were afraid, because it looked so black and the forests all around closed it off. They turned around and went back to their village at Hosma.

But in another month or two, they *took skin*, gathered their courage, and came back to Anggi with their families, their wives and children. The two men built houses at a place called Anuk, which is a little north of Sururay village, away from the Saiba clan. Two boys, Bau and I-jom-med-igo were born there.

At first, they lived in peace, but then men from the Saiba clan accused Inyomus of stealing their pigs. They hollered loudly and continually about it to Inyomus. It was so bad that both men took their families, and they all moved across the lake to live in Di-si-hu village. The Ijom and Indou families gave them land so they would stay there.

After that, they called Di-si-hu their home. When the old people and others in the family died, Inyomus ordered they all be buried (according to custom), across the lake.

But when Inyomus died, his son Bau brought his body back and placed it in the hollow trunk of the *in-yom-ste-ga* tree at Anuk. His bones stayed in the burial tree for many years—yes, several generations. But the tree with the ancestral bones grew old and dry and started to lean over. First, only one long bone fell from the hollow. A great-grandson, Wilem Inyomusi, and his wife, Loren, took the bone and stored it in their house near Anuk. The following year, a big wind blew the tree over and all of the grandfather's bones spilled on the ground. Again, Wilem and Loren carried the bones to their house and stored them, until the relatives gathered together to bury the remains in the ground near Wilem's house.

Nowadays the people are at peace and do not fight with each other. The Inyomusi grandchildren sleep in several places: some are in Disihu, others stay in Ransiki, and others dwell at I-jom-mur with the Hatam tribe.

Look back at the story:

1. What were Inyomus and Ihweij looking for when they first came to live by the lake?
2. What did the Saibas accuse Inyomus and Ihweij about?
3. When Inyomus died, where did they bury his bones?
4. Why do you think it was so important for the relatives to take care of Inyomus' bones when they fell out of the tree?

Burial tree with bones

Whistle for a Possum   Barbara Lunow

17. One of the very Old Ones, Grandfather Ijom-medigo from Disihu Village remembered the story of the first rafts on Anggi Lake. At first no one went on the lake, because they were afraid of the dense forests surrounding it. And they were terrified of creatures that might live in the dark, cold waters. No one knew how to swim, and they didn't want to try either. —Dessy

Inyomus and Ihweij Make a Raft
Grandfather Ijom-medigo, Disihu Village

Collecting Balsa wood for a raft

One day my Grandfathers Ihweij and Inyomus both thought of this in their hearts. They said to each other, "Let's go see what is at the lake's edge, over there in the water. There's something looking like a round stomach on top of the water."

53

So they searched in the forest and found three fat balsa trees, shaped like a barrel in the middle and thinner on the ends. They cut them down and tied them together with vines so that they could ride on them. They wanted to see what was on the water.

But they were also afraid of whatever was in the depths of the dark lake, because they were sure it wanted to try to take over their raft. They were afraid of other things about the water from the very first time they saw the lake. Things like: the eels, the ducks, and when the clouds rolled over the lake and made everything dark. That's why in the early days people didn't eat eel or ducks—they were afraid of them.

Next they made paddles something like this: At first they cut a straight, thin tree branch and they tried to row with it in the water. That didn't work very well. Later they made real paddles out of a wider branch from the *gowi* tree. They shaped it into a long shaft and made it wide and flat on one end.

I learned about all this from my father. He showed me how to make a raft and a paddle when I was a boy. In the early days, all of the trees to make these things were in the woods near the water's edge of Lake Anggi Giji. But now, in our time, it is more difficult. The trees for making rafts and paddles are far away from the shore and up in the forests on the mountain.

Think about the clans/families of the Sougb.

1. What took the two grandfathers so long before they made a raft?
2. List some things they were afraid of in the water?
3. How did they make the paddles?
4. Why is it harder to make rafts and paddles now?

18. *Listen to the voice of old Grandfather Ku-bay from Sun-gwa-dis village. He is one of the respected living grandfathers of our Sougb tribe. He was excited to tell some of the early stories to us, because he said no one wanted to hear them anymore. He wanted to tell about his clan, the Saibas, so that the children would know how they started to go out on rafts on Anggi Giji, Boy Lake, many years ago. They learned to make rafts long before they made dugout canoes with outriggers. — Dessy*

The Saiba Clan Makes a Raft
Grandfather Kubei Saiba, Sunggwadis Village

Making a raft

When we made a raft, the men went into the rain forest and searched for barrel shaped trees. These trees were close by at that time but are hard to find today. They cut three barrel-shaped trees and carried them to their house. They also collected rolls of vine from the forest.

The barrel tree is a balsa wood, shaped round, with no branches, and the insides are soft. First the men fastened three balsa wood trunks together with wooden pegs to make them strong. Then they tied them with vines and carried the raft down to the lake shore.

The first time they used the raft, one of my grandfathers *eic mos, put on skin,* (gathered his courage), and sat on it in the cold lake water to try it out. He balanced on it, pushing himself only a little way along the shore. And then he paddled with his hands and came back. The men decided it needed a little more vine tied around each end to make the raft more steady and secure.

When their hearts were satisfied that the raft was solid and firm, each man took a turn. They used their hands to paddle the raft along the shore by their village. This is as far as they went, because they were very afraid of the water in Lake Anggi Giji at that time. It took great courage to go on that first raft.

Making paddles for the rafts:

My people didn't make any paddles at first, because they didn't know how to do it yet. Time passed and they discovered how to make paddles from the *gowi* tree branches. They were happy, because with oars they could go around the lake and see things. There were many balsa and gowi trees growing in the forests all around the lake. They could make as many rafts and paddles as they wanted to make. At that time the people lived in their houses scattered on the mountainsides above the lake, because they were still afraid of the spirits in the water of Lake Anggi Giji.

Consider this:

1. The Sougb only use a certain kind of tree to make rafts. What are they called? Where are they located?
2. Describe their first ride on the lake.
3. What was the main thing they were afraid of in the lake?

19. *This story is from my grandmother's time in World War II, when she was a young girl. It is about when the Japanese soldiers came into our mountains looking for the Dutch soldiers. Nothing is made up; it is all true. Grandmother De-sing-may told us about it. Her village was over the mountains, on the other side of Anggi Lake. —Dessy*

When the Soldiers Came
Grandmother Desingmei Saiba, Trigdaga Village

I am Desingmay and this is my story, the way I remember it. I was a teenager when the soldiers from Japan came into our land. One day the Dutch soldiers ran from their post across the lake and came to a place not far from my village of Tes-tay-ga. They set up two large campsites there, because they were trying to hide from the Japanese soldiers who were looking for them.

The Sougb were afraid of the Japanese soldiers too. Many of them fled up the path through my village and climbed over the mountains to hide in Di-be-tig village. But some of the men stayed to help the Dutch soldiers and carry things for them. I was so afraid of all the soldiers that I stayed in my house and didn't run anywhere.

My uncle was the appointed chief of Dibetig. One day he brought several of his men and came down to the Dutch soldiers' camp. They fooled the Dutch by telling them, "The Japanese are coming."

The soldiers were so scared they ran away and left their stuff unguarded. My uncle and his men went quickly into the camps, stole their rice, and ran away.

When the Dutch soldiers finally returned and their rice was gone, they came and found us working in the gardens nearby. They took us and tied our hands together and questioned the men. Then they forced us all to march back to the village. We were scared, because before that time the foreigners had killed four Sougb men in the mountains. The soldiers put us in a fenced-in place, men and women separately, and guarded us with long guns.

I was terrified when they caught me. But then I remembered what the Dutch teacher who came before the war, told us about God. My heart believed some of what he said. So I prayed a little bit to God and asked Him to take care of me. Then one of my fathers, called U-bas, went to the soldiers and asked them to give me back, and they let me go with him. But the others in the fence, the Dutch killed them and threw their bodies into Anggi Lake. They also searched for my uncle and when they found him, they shot him.

After the Dutch soldiers killed my uncle and the other villagers, they left their camps and ran back to their post across the lake. Not long after that, they fled down the mountains from Anggi Giji Lake, all the way to Man-o-kwa-ree on the coast. Even when they left, we Sougb were still frightened all the time. So we left Anggi Lake and ran away into the mountains. We went to hide in the Dibetig and stayed there for a long time.

The Japanese military never found the Dutch soldiers in Anggi. They followed them down the pathways to the coast. We have a story that our Sougb men secretly shot one or two Japanese soldiers when they were fleeing our land. I am glad the soldiers left, but I am sorry they killed my uncle and other Sougb people.

Think about this:

1. The tribal people were afraid of the soldiers. They saw their supplies, especially the rice, and went into their camp and stole it. What would you have done?

2. Why do you think the soldiers let Desingmay go free?

3. How do you think the people could have protected themselves from the soldiers?

Culture, Customs of the Sougb People

Man carrying Black Magic poisons

20. *In the old days my people built houses using only natural materials they found in the rain forest and the jungle. Now they build many houses out of sawn lumber or cement blocks. They make the roof out of sheets of zinc, which is very noisy when it rains. This story tells how to build a house the traditional way. The grandfathers felt proud when they built their own houses. —Dessy*

Poles, Bark, and Thatch
Martinus Saiba, Sururay Village

Traditional house

Constructing the bark outer wall

Sewing the palm frond roof

Smoke-sealing the new roof

Women by the fireside

Fire-side sleeping pole

My name is Martinus and I like to work with my hands. When I was a boy, my father taught me how to make a bow and arrow and to erect a bamboo fence. I also watched and learned from my father and uncles how to build a Sougb house. When our old house, *tu mohon,* was falling down, my father, older brother and I began collecting materials for a *tu menau,* new house. It took us several months to get everything together.

This is how we make our traditional houses even today: First, we go to the rain forest and look for trees large enough for a man to stretch his arms around to use for foundation poles. Each one must be thick and have a fork in it to hold up the flooring poles and external walls of the house. Then we collect the vines, *aig-da-ga,* and cut them down from the trees so we can tie our house together. We wrap the vine into rolls and store them until they are needed.

The next part is for the women. My mother and aunts clear a patch of ground which must be big enough for us to build a small storage hut for the things we own and also a lean-to to sleep in while the new house is being built. Then men climb up and tear off the palm-leaf roofing on the old house to cover the two huts. The women dig a small fireplace pit in the lean-to so we can cook and be warmer when we sleep near it on the ground.

For the new house, the men and young boys of the family use vines to measure off a rectangular space, which is normally close to the old one. We start by digging a center hole, with other holes around the outer edge of the new site. Then we take the main foundation log, called the *buch man-day-ch,* and stand it straight up on top of a large flat rock that was placed in the bottom of the center hole. They pack around the pole so that it will stand firmly. Then we place *go-hob,* foundation logs, in the other holes and pack them in the same way. The main frame for the flooring is built above the ground, from five to eight feet high. The poles for the floor rest in the forks of the foundation timbers. Floor supports from stripped branches, are crisscrossed, layered, and tied together with vine so they remain strong and firm.

The skeleton frame, *tu med-go-mor-ee,* which marks the outside of the house and the inside room divisions, is made by stripping bark from smaller branches and securing them upright to the floor supports and the foundation poles. We cross over two or three times with these branches to strengthen the framework. Then we add the main ridge for the peak of the roof with the cross poles over that. We wrap the vines around and the joints to hold everything together. After all the frame poles are tied, we are ready to seal the house from rain.

It is the men's job to make the roofing, *uf,* from a special palm leaf that we collect in the jungle, or sometimes on the mountain. When it's gathered, the women slice the stickers off the edges of the palm fronds and quickly drag the leaves through an open fire to soften and bend them. Then the men sew the folded fronds over a bamboo pole to make a section of roofing. They use a thorn needle and bark string made by the women. Lastly, they tie each palm leaf section, in overlapping layers, on the roof poles. After the roof is on, the men attach young tree branches in cross-poles all around the outside framework of the house. For the walls, they fasten sheets of tree bark, or si-beej, to the frame.

Inside the house, the men divide the left side of the house and make small sleeping rooms with bark walls for the women of the family, but the right side is left open for the men. Then we make clay fireplaces, *hirog,* for the wood fires.

The women bring in the clay to stomp in the fireplaces, for their own fires and also for the men's fireplace. The men place a pillow-pole across the divide between the flooring and clay fireplace. This pole goes the length of the house and is used to rest the head on for sleeping. The same type of pole is placed in front of each of the fireplaces in the women's rooms also. A sleeping rack, or storage rack, is built above the fireplace on the men's side, against the wall. For the floor, we strip a thick, smooth bark in long, wide sheets off a special tree and cover over the flooring framework of the house.

The last step is to cut down a tree and use the trunk to make a pole to climb up into the house *ig-dech-gwa.* We chop notches in the trunk for footholds. Before we sleep in the new house we build fires out of young saplings so that the smoke will coat the rafters and waterproof the roof. We burn those fires for a couple of days before we move in. Finally, we can live in the new house.

If we have collected all the materials ahead of time, and there are three or four builders, it takes about three to four weeks to build a house.

It is the father's duty to instruct his sons in building a house. He shows them how to make palm roofing, where to get the good jungle vines, find poles for the frame, and which trees are best for their bark. He warns them that they must know how to build their own houses, because one day in the future he will not be able to help them. As I learned from my father, so the mothers also teach the daughters their duties in helping to build a new house. We Sougb are proud to build our own houses from materials in the jungle and forest.

Consider this: Sougb men and women have traditional duties, passed down from generation to generation, for building a Sougb house.

1. What are the duties for the men and boys?
2. What are the duties for the women and girls?
3. What are some of the raw materials that they use to build their houses?
4. Could you build a Sougb house from the directions that Martinus gave? Explain how you might do it.

21. Gardens are very important because we grow our own food and would have little to eat otherwise. Our main foods are sweet potato and white potato. To make money for buying other things, we have small garden plots containing only shallot onions and garlic. It is hard work making a garden, but it is also a fun time when all the family gets together. The children especially like it, because when they clean out the weeds and bushes from the ground there are bonfires spread all over the garden. Everyone uses the fires to burn off weeds and brush, but the children use them to sit around and bake their sweet potatoes in the ashes any time they want to. —Dessy

How Does Your Garden Grow?
Widow Sdemos Ahoren, Sagwameba Village

Going to the garden

Before we start a new garden, we must wait for the whole family to come together. The important ones who need to be there are the brothers and sisters, parents and grandparents. They all own pieces of the land for the gardens. Sometimes we wait for a long time for someone to come back from town on the coast.

When the family is finally gathered, we women clear the land of weeds, brush and bushes. Then my sons and the other men cut down the big trees, which they will let dry out and use for firewood later. The men gather young trees and branches to build a split-pole fence around the garden. The fence is to keep our pigs out. We wait a week or more for all the brush to dry and then we burn it all off inside the fence. The men take vines and sticks to divide and mark off sections for everyone.

After the ground is prepared and burned off, the adult relatives and their children plant their sections. Each one carries a stick, or a steel rod, and we go all over the sections digging holes to plant the seeds. They are planted in the following order: first we plant the squash seeds, then we cut up pieces of white potatoes and throw them in the little holes, next are several corn seeds to a hole, then green bean seeds, and finally we plant the sweet potato vines. We make special holes, a little bigger, for the vine stalk and pack the dirt around the vine. Then we are done.

I am a widow, but I am also allowed sections of the garden to plant for myself. I always set aside a part of my plot for growing potatoes to feed the clinic workers and church leaders who stay in my house when they come for new supplies and teaching.

We wait and wait for the seeds to grow and hope for rain. In about two weeks the beans sprout. Then the potatoes begin to grow, with the green bush or vines above ground and the potatoes underground. The green beans grow and mature quickly. They are the first harvest. The corn doesn't fully ripen until about five months and the potatoes about the same time, or longer.

When the corn is yellow-orange, I call for my children, "Everybody come now and feast on corn with me." After we eat the young, moist corn, we hang mature corn ears to dry in the house for replanting the seeds again.

Then the white potatoes are mature, and I call my children again, "Everybody come now, because I see the potatoes are ready to eat." But we leave the section for the clinic workers and church leaders. We dare not eat from their harvest. We will wait for them to come.

The sweet potatoes keep growing after the vegetables are gone. We can eat on them for about a year. Then we have to make a new garden.

In order to clear a garden, we let the pigs eat all the leftover sweet potatoes in the old garden. The pigs clean it out and root up the soil while they eat. Then we can plant onions and more white potatoes in that space.

After we take the pigs out, the old garden plot is left to stand before we make it into a new garden again. We must wait several years and let the young trees grow first. When the new trees are tall, it's time to clear the land and plant another garden.

Building a garden fence

Consider these questions:

Most of the work in planting a garden and harvesting the crops is women's work.

1. What do the men do to get a new garden ready?
2. How do the Sougb plant their gardens?
   Compare that to how you would plant the seeds.
3. What is the unique way that the Sougb use to dig up the garden after the harvest is gone?

22. Father told me how it was before the yellow-skin and white-skin people came to our land. Sougb men and women wore their hair long, and did not cut it very often. They styled it in ways that are different from today. I know an old grandfather who still wears his hair long, in the old way. Also, in earliest times, the Sougb did not have clothes. They only wore a loincloth, which covered their private body parts. Much later the men wore shorts and the women had wrap around sarong cloths. — Dessy

Fashion and Fancy
Mama Desijohota Saiba, Sunggwadis Village

Men and women in our grandfathers' time liked to *e-krees*, braid, their hair. Certain ones of their friends were skillful in doing this. The men wound their braids around their heads. The women made many braids down the back of their heads. Sometimes they took the braids out to work in the garden, and left it all bushed out. After a while, they folded it back into braids again.

Hair styles for the men

In the old times, the men never cut their hair. It hung down to their shoulders in matted, tight curls or in braids. They often gathered the loose hair in bunches and tied it with bark string. A trusted friend, who was clever in fixing hair, wove the braids in special designs. Once it was braided, they left it like that and never washed it. It is also true, in those days no one ever bathed their whole body either so their skin looked much darker and dirtier than it does now.

Some men were artistic and carved wide bamboo picks with different geometric designs. The patterns had no special meaning. The men stuck the combs in their hair in the back of their heads, thinking they looked good, and to show off to the girls.

Everyone had head lice at some time or other but they still did not cut their hair. Instead, the medicine man, who knew of such things, went out into the jungle and the rain forest to find certain plants, such as tobacco leaves, to make a poison to kill the lice. They left these remedies to soak into their scalp.

When a baby was born, the mother might choose to cut her hair. She wove whatever she cut off into a wide band, called a g-string belt, and tied it around the baby's middle, below the waist. The parents used their own hair to show the child belonged to them. The child wore this waist belt for several years. No one else could give their hair because the parents and grandparents feared someone else's hair might be used in sorcery to harm the child.

Picking head lice lineup

Men's clothing and decoration

In the earliest of days, the grandfathers pounded the inside bark of a certain tree into a soft strip and made a loincloth (a covering for their private parts). When they discovered the red material from the trading ships, the men used it for their loincloths. The women's cloth was always black or deep blue. They took three to four yards of material and folded it over into a long narrow strip of cloth and then wrapped it around their waists, leaving a tail hanging in back. Then they pulled the tail between their legs and tucked the end into the wrap-around waistcloth in the front. The men wore their loincloths everywhere without shame, because they believed they were properly dressed.

The men and women also used dog teeth to make necklaces. Or they strung other animal teeth (tree kangaroo, wild pig tusks) with their beads and wore them.

Special adornments were required for certain occasions: a feast, a dance, a black magic or sorcery ritual, or preparing for war. At those times, the men and women wore rare glass-bead necklaces, wide and narrow etched, shell armbands, and shell disks in their hair, or tied around their head and hung on the forehead. The shell armbands were worn like bracelets above the elbow. They also crisscrossed long woven strips of bark string with attached cowry shells over their chests. The beads and shells came from foreign traders on the ships.

Young man in loincloth

Women's hair styles

In the old days, the women wore their hair long, the same as the men. But they styled it in different patterns of braids. They pulled some of their long hair forward into a bunch on their foreheads. A trusted friend tied the bundle together with bark string, and placed a flat, carved shell disk on top of the hair knot. The disks were valuable, because they were so rare. If a woman had one, she was proud to wear it in her hair, like it was a precious coin.

Women's clothing and decorations

Like the men, women did not wear clothes. They only wore a wide band around their hips, below the belly button, called a g-string. These belts were woven from yellow and black orchid fibers. Sometimes they mixed strands of their hair into the bands. They attached a piece of dark blue or black cloth as a loincloth. The women's cloth was only long enough to go between the legs. The men traded with the strangers in the sailing ships for the women's cloth. The women never traded for themselves. Nowadays most men and women have at least one pair of underwear that they wear to church, or for going to town. Otherwise, they still wear the loincloth and g-string.

The women also wore jewelry. The multi-strand necklaces of red and yellow glass beads were the most common and every woman had at least one set. The bead necklaces were heavy but the women wore them every day, even when working in the gardens. They also had other special beads and shell armbands which they wore to dances and ceremonies in preparation for war. Beads of other colors were saved for dowry payments. They were more expensive because they were rare. We can't buy them at all today. The women also wore the woven cowry-shell strips draped across their breasts. A few had earrings, which were made from pieces of brass or a nail, and the men bent them into curved shapes to put into a hole in the earlobe.

In long ago times, they used bark blankets to cover themselves at night and stay warm. The women took *sogo mos, tree skin,* and pounded it into bark blankets. This was before the traders brought wrap-around sarongs for them to wear and use as a covering at night. Now we buy real blankets from the market or the stores in town on the coast. Our favorite colors are red with a black stripe.

Little girl wearing a g-string

Tattoos for women

The women liked to tattoo their cheeks, foreheads, upper arms, and sometimes across their abdomen. A friend drew geometric patterns with ash from the fires and then pricked the design into the skin with thorns. While it was still bleeding, they rubbed more ashes or wild berry juice, mixed with spit, into the wounds to make different colors. The tattoos didn't mean anything—they just liked tattoos. Sometimes the new tattoos got infected before they healed over.

Unmarried girls also liked to have beauty scars on their stomachs. A girlfriend pricked the design into their skin, mostly shaped liked the mountain pathways in zig-zags. Then she rubbed ashes into the wound, and spit on it to make the scars puffy. This was more dangerous, because the wounds broke open and started to bleed, or the sores wouldn't heal.

There were certain women who were known for being artful in making the tattoo-scars. If a girl went to her, the woman cut the design, and she stayed at the woman's house for about two weeks, until the scars healed over. The one who

performed the scarring watched over her and put herbal medicine on the wounds. Unmarried girls had scars across their abdomens just because they thought they were pretty. I have these scars on my stomach, too.

Think about this and compare the old styles to now:

1. Tell about the hairstyles of men and women? Can you braid your hair like they did?
2. What color loincloth did the men wear? The women?
3. What about blankets from generations ago? Blankets now?

23. *We Sougb like tattoos, for fun and for beauty. Teenage girls tattoo their faces, only they draw smaller designs now. I already told about tattoos for decoration, but in this story Grandfather Yonaden tells more about tattooing from the old days. — Dessy*

Beauty and Disguise
Grandfather Yonaden Ahoren, Kofo Village

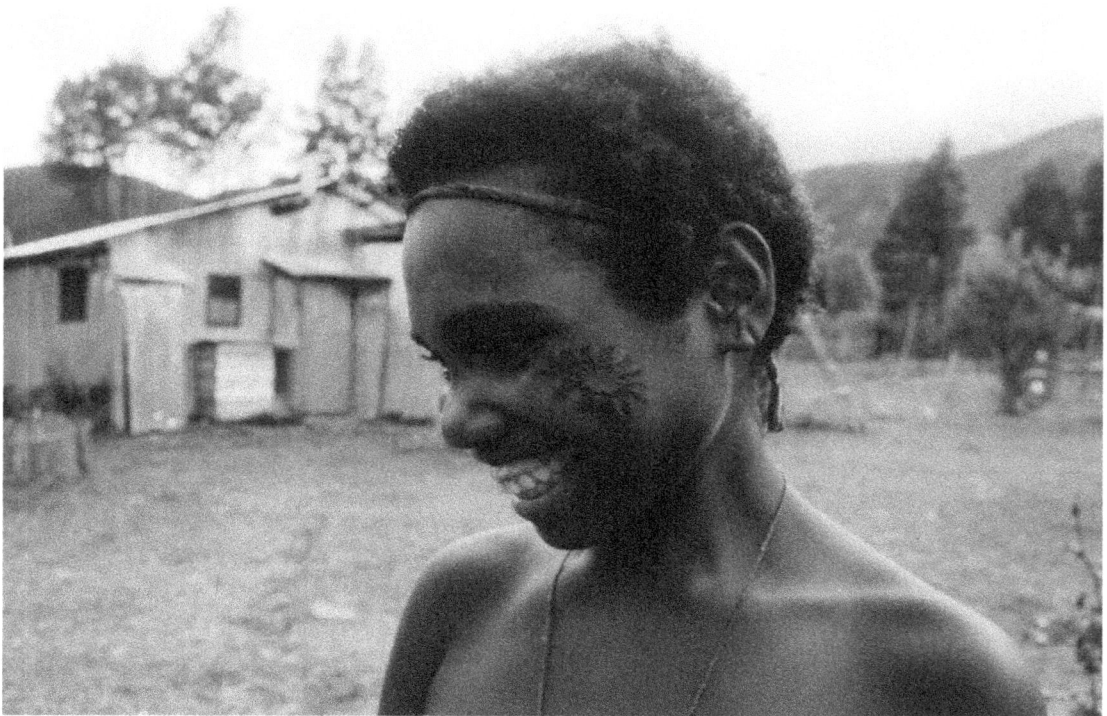

Young girl with facial tattoo

In the old days our grandfathers and grandmothers tattooed their faces. To make the tattoo, they first looked for a long thorn from the lemon tree. Using the thorn, they poked a design on the face, deep enough to make it bleed. One design looked like the lines of the bark from a certain tree. Another common pattern was like the *los mo-ho-ra*, rain legs, looking like streaks of rain. After a while, the tattoos turned to a dark blue or purple color.

The meaning of tattoos

The girls and boys thought they would attract each other with their beauty marks. The unmarried girls thought that tattoos would make them prettier so their fathers could ask for a higher bride price in their marriage arrangements. This is what the women did.

For the boy, besides making himself more handsome, a young warrior had tattoos for disguise. Our ancestors were always fighting with other clans. They tried to hide from their enemies by disguising their faces with tattoos. They thought the enemy wouldn't know them and be afraid of them. At the same time, their friends recognized the designs on their faces and knew who they were.

Think about this: The men and women originally wore no clothing, but there were distinctive differences in their loincloths, and the way they decorated their hair and drew tattoos.

1. What is the meaning of tattoos?
2. How do the Sougb make tattoos?
3. How are tattoos made in western countries?
4. Why do people get tattoos in America?

24. We love our pigs. We treat them like our children, naming each one, and carrying them around in our arms when they are piglets. It is important to us that we feed and take care of them so they will grow big, strong and be more valuable. In my culture pigs are like money. We use them to trade for other goods and to make payments. This story is from old Grandfather Ho-da Dou-an-si-ba who lived across the lake from my village. He was more than 80 years-old when he told this story. His eyes were blind, but his mind was clear and he was excited to tell the tales from his childhood. —Dessy

Pigs are Precious
Grandfather Hoda Douansiba, Irai village

A long time ago a man named Ug-da-ren bought a pig near the seashore and brought it up to the mountains. It was the very first pig in our land. Later on another man named Ma-nu-gwo bought a pig from Ugdaren. After that Ugdaren bought more pigs from the foreigners down by the seashore. These foreigners had real guns. They tended their pigs in a fenced-in pasture on the flat land by the sea. They lived close to the coastal towns of Ransiki and Momi in the district of Manokwaree.

I know this story, because Ugdaren was my great-uncle of long ago. But I called Manugwo like my older brother. These two men were both from the Douansiba family clan.

From that time on, we Sougb raised many pigs here in the mountains. We built fences of tree poles around our sweet potato gardens, but the pigs were free to wander around inside and outside of the fences. It was okay because there was much food for all of us and for the pigs to eat too. In fact, when the Sougb weren't at war, we ate pig meat all the time.

But now the government officials tell us there is pig dirt everywhere: close to our houses, in the yards, in the water and on the trails. They tell us we have to make fences for the pigs, otherwise we will get very sick. It is hard for the women because if the pigs are fenced up they must dig sweet potatoes to bring to them. Inside the pens the pigs do not fatten quickly. Sometimes their bodies are sickly and they die. The ones that live are always small.

Today we don't keep so many pigs. There are only enough to roast pork for a feast maybe two or three times a year. We might kill pigs to celebrate when someone collects a bridal payment, or for the third night of mourning to remember someone who died. Sometimes we have a holiday feast, like for Christmas or New Year's. Our hearts are sad because we don't have enough pigs to have a pig feast very often.

1. Where did the Sougb first get their pigs?
2. Why did the government officials make them change the way they tended their pigs?
3. Why didn't the Sougb want to fence their pigs in?
4. What are some differences between the Sougb way and the western way of raising pigs?

25. *Grandfather Hoda was so happy to talk about the old days. At first he forgot things, but when he talked, he remembered. These are about our culture and things we were still afraid of in my father and mother's time. —Dessy*

Taboos and Customs for Pig

Lap piggy

Pigs, for Payment or Bride Price (Dowry):

When I was young, I took care of my pigs so I could use them to buy or trade for bridal cloth, beads and shell armbands. Then I could marry a wife. One shell armband cost me a piglet. But when I bought a long piece of cloth I had to trade a grown mother pig, about three or four years old. I went around to my relatives to trade my pigs for the bridal goods. Years later, I helped my son pay for his wife and I had to give three or four grown pigs for each piece of cloth. The bride's family also asked me to give them cloth, strings of glass-beads, and carved shell armbands. All of this went to the girl's father and her relatives as payment so I could bring her to my son for his bride.

Pigs, When the Sougb Fought a War:

In the old days, the Sougb fought with each other continually. One day when they grew tired of war, they called for a truce and traded/gave a pig to the enemy so they would examine their hearts and negotiate for peace. When all the men agreed to end a war, they exchanged many pigs, which they killed and cooked for a feast. According to our custom, the Big Heads, or the chiefs of the clans, divided the pork out among all the men who were fighting. Then both sides sat down and ate together. This showed everyone that their hearts were in accord, they were united as one. Their disagreements and differences were settled, they made peace.

Pigs, Bowing Down to the Pig's Spirit:

In the past, the Sougb used pigs in worship. They bowed down and prayed to them, like an idol, hoping they would be protected from evil, or get good things. When a person was sick, they killed a pig. Their friends took the blood and spread it over the sick one's body and on his chest. They also took a little piece of cooked pork in a small pot to the sick person for him to eat first. They cut a small piece of meat to place over the doorway so the *min-di-ree* -spirits or ghosts of the dead, would not harm the sick person again. Afterwards the others in the house ate the rest of the pork.

Women were afraid of pigs when they had a new baby. They believed that the child would die if the pig ate its spirit. Because of this fear the new mother did not tend to the pigs immediately after giving birth. She waited until her baby started to crawl, then she felt it was safe to take care of the pigs again.

Riding piggy-back

Consider the importance of pigs in the Sougb culture:

1. How are pigs used in the bride price system?
2. How are pigs used in a peace agreement for a war?
3. How did the Sougb use pig's blood to pray?
4. Why was a new mother with a baby afraid of pigs?

26. *When I am fifteen or sixteen, I will get married. My father and uncles will choose a husband for me and arrange my marriage. Some of my friends say that their fathers picked a boy for them to marry when they were babies. No matter what age we are married, there will be a huge payment made to our fathers and uncles. This has been our practice for generations.*

This story tells about the cloth that is used for bride price, or dowry payment. Most of the cloth is very old and only three of the great-grandfathers that I know can recite all the names of the grandfathers and the cloth from the earliest generations down to my time now. They recite from memory the names of the clans who traded for the cloth and when they got it. It is sad, but today I do not know of any young person who has this information stored in his heart. —Dessy

Piles and Piles of Cloth
Harun Inden, Nenay Village

Displaying dowry cloth

In the old days my people used the cloth from the East brought by foreign sailing ships for economic settlements in cultural affairs. We used the cloth for marriage arrangements, to pay when accused of using witchcraft or black magic, making peace in a war, and for other village happenings.

When my grandfathers first owned cloth, they traded it from men of the island of Timor, the *Bom-joh*. These foreigners came to our land to find tropical bird feathers and tobacco. They traded the *Kain Timor* cloth to my grandfathers for these things. In those days the In-den clan lived in the Bin-tu-nee area. Later, the *Sig-bay-na* tribe also started trading for cloth, and then they traded it down through the generations to all of us.

One of my grandfather's most valuable pieces he called *minch menau, new cloth*. But in my generation it is already very old cloth. Its colors are black and white with a little red woven in. The black design was named after a curling, leafy fern. The white was the shape of a feather. The design in between the black was named after a flower. My grandfather's cloth was fringed on the ends with colored bird feathers, pig tails and dried seed pods. He also fastened a piece of furry possum skin in the middle.

It was important to know the size of each piece of the woven cloth and the length of each bolt of fabric. They measured the length of the woven cloth from a man's chin down to his feet. The width was measured by a man's out-stretched arms. When they used the cloth for payment, they remembered the length, width, and design so that the same piece of cloth would not be given back to them in the future. Also, the value of the cloth was determined by size, color, and design.

Measuring the length of the dowry cloth

My grandfathers stored the cloth in a hand-beaten bark blanket that was tied with vine. After tying and wrapping it, they put it away on a bamboo shelf in their houses. The Sougb always tried to collect more cloth. It was like money stored away and showed how rich they were. They placed the best pieces of cloth on the bottom of the pile and the cheaper ones on top, in case anyone tried to look at the cloth. Now, in my time, we store the fabric in rice sacks, in wooden storage boxes, or in large suitcases so outsiders coming into our houses cannot see how much we have.

In the past there were fewer Sougb people, and we had more cloth. But now we have more people, and there is less cloth for trade and making payments. The old cloth is very valuable because you cannot buy it anymore. The new bolts of cloth are cheaper, because anyone can buy them in stores. The Sougb economic system is still based on cloth and beads.

Dowry goods displayed inside the house

Think about this:

1. What items are required for the Sougb economic system?
2. Where did the Sougb originally get their woven cloth?
3. How can they get it now? Where?
4. What are the two main purposes for collecting cloth?

27. In our grandfathers' time, my people didn't have paper or coin money. Instead, we traded goods with each other. This story is about the bead necklaces that we use for dowry (marriage) payments and other settlements. The trade and slave ships no longer sail, which means it is not possible to get glass beads anymore. Each household treasures and still uses the old beads and now they are considered very valuable. Mostly they are stored in our houses to use when a payment is made. Women no longer wear big clusters of them for every day. Most women have at least one strand that they wear all the time. —Dessy

More Than a Necklace
Grandfather Yonaden Ahoren, Kofo Village

Woman wearing glass dowry beads

A very long time ago, the Sougb men traded for rare ocean pearls, and glass or Chinese lacquered beads from foreigners who came in sailing ships to our shores. The men on these ships were looking for the Bird of Paradise feathers that the Sougb hunted for them. When the Dutch came to settle in our land many years later, we traded fresh produce for cheaper beads from the store owners who lived in the coastal towns of Papua.

The women wore common red and yellow glass beads in long strands over their bare breasts. They tied as many as eight or ten strands together. The necklaces were heavy, especially when the women worked in the gardens. These common beads were called *lee-mo-go*.

The older beads were stored away and kept for special times: wearing them at the dances before going to war or in black magic rituals. They used beads to exchange in ceremonies for bridal payments or as a settlement in other affairs. The men wore beads in one or two strands over their red loincloths, or they fastened beads and a pearl on the g-string belts below their hips. Men no longer wear beads and women only wear one or two strands, like a necklace, for decoration.

We also use carved shells as armbands and ornaments to tie around the forehead. These shells are old, going back to early generations; maybe 150-200 years old.

abaga = white, round shell, cut crossways, made into armbands, carved with lines and small circles, worn on the upper arm all the time. The Sougb didn't have tools or metal knives to decorate them. The sailors on ships carved them and traded them with my people.

amplok = from the coast, no longer available, icicle shaped shell, beige-brown color. Hole in top and tied around forehead. Old men wore them all the time, but younger men only wore them for feasts and dancing.

Think about this:
1. Where did the Sougb get their beads?
2. How were they originally used?
3. How are they used today?
4. How old are some of them?

28.   *In generations past, the Sougb people treasured three things above everything else: our pigs, the bridal cloth and our beads. A man who had stored up these things was considered rich. They are still important to the economy today and are used for marriage payments and for settlement in other tribal affairs. In my lifetime we Sougb are learning of a more precious treasure than our pigs, cloth and beads. My pastor told about it in our Sunday House when he gave some beads to the ones who brought us the voice of God, the Sougb New Testament. —Dessy*

Beads of Mankind
Pastor Yonaden Ahoren, Kofo Village

Pastor Yonaden held up a string of dowry beads: white, black, red and yellow for everyone to see. He reminded us, "In our grandfathers' time, before the white-skins came, we Sougb lived by ourselves. We were just like the beads on this necklace, but we were scattered all over. We had nothing to hold us together. People were living their own lives, each man to himself, doing his own thing.

Then the white-skins came, bringing God's voice, bringing us Jesus. Jesus is the string that unites us, and the Holy Spirit is the knot that ties us all together. But I want to show you now that it isn't just white-skins on the string, but also black-skins like us. See, there are red-skins, and yellow-skins too."

After showing us the single strand of colored beads, he took three clusters of many strands of our valuable dowry beads and held them up for all to see. Each cluster also had a single strand of the black, white, red, and yellow beads attached to it.

Pastor Yonaden took beads of many strands and placed a necklace over each missionary's head. He gave a speech, saying to them, "We thank you, *Tuan*, Missionary Lunow, because you are like the spring which brings forth clean, pure water. You are always working to change God's voice into our Sougb voice, and teaching us the meaning of it.

We thank you, *Nyonya,* Mrs. Barbara, and *Nona,* Miss Pat, because you are like a freely flowing stream that gives clean water and life. *Ibu Barbara,* you bring us Sunday Schools for our children and Bible classes for our widows. *Nona Pat,* you taught us at the Bible School all these years. We also thank you because you are both like pools, always brimming to overflowing, bringing medicine and health, and life to our sick bodies.

And now, with the beads of our dowry, which are worth very little, we are also giving each of you one string of these Beads of Mankind. Each string has beads of black, white, red, and yellow. Take our necklaces with you and show your people, the ones who sent you. Tell them that it is no longer only the white-skins on the string but now we Sougb, with blackskins, are also on the string. Tell them thank you from the Sougb people.

Now, we are all one. We are the same, all blood drops, truly the adopted children of God."

Think about this: The story uses dowry necklaces as a new symbol for beads belonging to all of mankind.

1. What does the single attached string stand for?
2. What about the knot?
3. What do the different colored beads represent?

29. *Grandmother Dobmoro sat by her fire and told us about her life as a young woman in the Sougb tribe. She was very old, but she remembered everything about how it was in our culture long ago. She told us about getting married, the duties of a wife and having a baby. —Dessy*

Wedding Planners
Grandmother Dobmoro Saiba, Sururay Village

Marriages were always arranged for a daughter. My father was a Big Head in our clan, so he asked for a huge bride price for his daughters.

The young man's father, with other male relatives, came to our house and told my dad, "I want to take your daughter to my son." They also brought bridal cloth and other dowry goods with them to give to him.

When they all agreed on the bride price the two fathers made pledges to each other at our house.

The boy's father told my father, "I will take your daughter for my son."

My father replied, "There is nothing, no disagreement or discontent, between you and me. You can come and take her."

Another day they brought the dowry payment and spread it out in a long line from the inside of the house to the outside. Everyone came by the house to see it displayed. When the dowry payment was accepted and the fathers repeated the pledge to each other, they shook hands. The boy's father, my new father-in-law, took me to his house. It was a procession, with me in front and people following behind singing and chanting as we marched along the way.

After I lived in my in-law's house for a while and my mother-in-law approved of all my work, the men brought an even larger dowry payment to my father's house. The goods were like the first installment: bolts of cloth, shell armbands, bead necklaces, and live pigs. This time no one sang about the payment. Instead, my father and uncles spoke disdainfully about it. They were trying to get more out of the in-laws by pointing out how cheap they thought their payment was. They talked like this, saying,

"Are these shell armbands?'"

"You call these bead necklaces?"

"Is this supposed to be good cloth? How long is it? How wide?"

"Look at these pigs. They're too skinny. Where is the suckling sow and her piglets?"

By the time of the second payment I had already stayed in my husband's family house for months. After arguing back and forth, the goods were finally accepted, and my father divided it up with my relatives who carried their share home with them.

A payment in cloth was also made when I had my first child. My dad and uncles were given more goods again. All together, there were as many as 200 pieces of cloth piled high in my father's house. This is true because I saw it with my own eyes. I was always proud that the bride price for me was so big.

My family name is an important one, so my father asked a lot for me. I never got any of the goods for myself except for a couple of yards (one meter is thirty-nine inches) of cloth to make a sarong to wear once in a while. The goods were for the men in my family. That is the way it was.

Compare differences between a tribal wedding and western wedding:

1. Name four differences between the tribal and western weddings.

2. Which wedding/marriage would you like best? Why?

30. *Girls in our tribe are taught their place and what is expected of them as early as when they learn to walk and talk. The mothers, aunts and grandmothers take them to the gardens to work and learn how to watch younger brothers and sisters. I too was taught these things. When I was a teenager, my mother died—I had to raise my baby brother. Grandmother Dobmoro told us about her duties after she was married. —Dessy*

Work, Work, Work
Grandmother Dobmoro Saiba, Sururay Village

Sorting dried beans for a new garden

We girls were taught to work as soon as we could walk. First, we fed the pigs. We went with our mothers and aunts to work in the gardens, planting and digging sweet potatoes. When we were older we watched over the younger children and carried them on our backs. Our duties also included bringing home firewood and hauling drinking water in a gourd. Every day, we had this work to do, always. Learning these things prepared us for life.

When we were in our teens, our fathers and uncles arranged our marriages. Sometimes marriages were decided when the boy and girl were just babies. The girl did not have a choice in the one she was to marry.

As I got older and was still in my father's house, my parents instructed me on my behavior in my future in-laws' house.

"Be sure you cook really good for them."

"Be generous to your husband's relatives and feed them also. "

"Work diligently in the garden so you have enough food. "

"Tend to their pigs so that not one dies. "

"Give food with an open hand to the orphans and poor, those that come to your house."

Women cleared and burned brush for a new garden. The men felled trees and built garden fences. Women planted sweet potato vines and many other seeds. We weeded it all after the plants started to grow. By tending the gardens every day, we always had enough to eat at harvest time.

When I worked diligently for my in-laws, they gave bundles of dowry cloth to my father and uncles. This is true. I really saw this in my parents' house.
My heart was proud to be worth so much dowry.

Compare the differences again:

1. Name three things expected of a Sougb wife?

   A western wife?

2. Which one do you like better? Why?

31. *Grandmother Dob-mo-ro was not afraid to tell us about having babies when she was a young wife. Traditions were the same for all Sougb women. But now, the women are allowed to help each other and we do not have to follow the taboos and rules when I was a young mother. I'm glad those things have changed in my lifetime. —Dessy*

It's a Boy or a Girl
Grandmother Dobmoro Saiba, Sururay Village

While I had a *stomach already* (was pregnant), I still worked in the gardens every day. I cleared the land for a new garden, planted sweet potato vines, corn and beans. I also fed the pigs, worked in the garden, carried water and brought home firewood. I did not sit around.

When I had my babies in the *little* house (the *birthing* hut), I stayed in it for about a week after my children were born. My mother was allowed to cook food and bring it to me. After I came out of the birth-hut, I climbed up the notched pole to the big house to my little room there. No one helped me either. I had to dig my own sweet potatoes and cook them. I drew water and carried my own firewood. It was custom for the new mother to do everything for herself. I had all my eight children in this way.

My in-laws also expected that I go back to work in their gardens as quickly as possible after coming up to the big house. I shared fresh food from the garden with the other family members living in our house. Sometimes I strapped the baby to my back and worked. Other times my mother-in-law watched my infant and also helped me in the garden. I breast-fed my babies and when they could crawl, I alone cooked sweet potatoes for them. Other mothers allowed their sisters to feed their babies, but I didn't.

These are taboos and things forbidden during the time we have a stomach:
1. When a woman has a stomach (is pregnant), her father and uncles warn her against eating certain foods, so she will not lose the baby. They warn against foods like possum which a dog hunted, wild pork and deer. Also she is not to eat corn or eggs.

92

2. If she wants to get a stomach, or not lose her baby when she is pregnant, a woman must not go in front of strangers on the trail. It is feared they might use black magic from their net bag and cast a spell on her; thus making her sick, or her stomach will hurt, and she will go into labor and lose the baby.

Taboos, things forbidden for new baby and mother:

1. A new mother and her baby are not allowed to eat in someone else's house, or at their fire, because it is feared the child might get sick and die.
2. The new mother can only eat whatever she cooks for herself.
3. It is not allowed for the new mother to drink the creek water anymore.
4. The new mother cannot get vegetables from the little garden that is planted under the house. This ground is considered unclean because the pigs and chickens live under the houses.
5. When a woman brings her baby from the birthing house up to the big house, she must stay inside for two days. If she walks on the ground, a pig might eat the baby's spirit and the baby will die. Or a pig might eat the mother's spirit and she will die.
6. The baby is also forbidden certain foods: banana, papaya, and corn. The baby could die if the mother feeds it those foods. But if she waits until the baby crawls, then she can feed baby the forbidden food and the mother can also eat them.

Think about these things and compare them to what you know in our country:

1. What is a taboo?
2. Why do you think the new mother followed so many taboos?
3. Would you follow them? Explain why.
4. What kind of rules do we have in our society for expectant mothers and new babies?
5. Why do we have these rules?

32. Our mothers tell us to take care of the old people. But sometimes they are left alone in an old home where the roof leaks and the house is falling down. That is not good because their children are not showing them respect. These rules that I share with you are from our ancestors and they are always true and right. I believe we must still follow them today. —Dessy

Grandmas and Grandpas
Mama Desijohota Saiba, Sunggwadis Village

Old Man Kubay by his fireside

Adult people build their own houses. If the parents are older but still able to take care of themselves, they live alone. It is the children's duty to help them repair their houses or build new ones. But when a grandfather or grandmother is really old they will *eig-tou de-sij* (sit next to, stay) with one of their children.

As a parent gets old and weak or sick, one of their adult children makes a small sleeping room in his house for them. The room is barely big enough for a fireplace and for the old person to enter and sleep by himself. The old grandfather's room is at the far end of the men's side, and the grandma's room is on the far end of the women's side. The old one wants to be separate from the family because they are afraid they might get a cough or have runny eyes.

The grandma, especially, says her heart would worry about sleeping near the younger women and children in their room.

When the room partition is added in the back of the house, the old one enters into it for always—the rest of their life. The son or daughter, and grandchildren watch over them. Every day they bring the respected one sweet potatoes, greens, water and firewood.

When my mother's mother was very old, she came to live with us. My mother gave me these instructions, saying:

"Watch over your grandmother really well. We will keep her with us now because Grandmother is very old already and unable to help herself. That is why you must be diligent to watch over her and take care of her. She must eat beside her own fire so we don't get sick from her. If she eats by our fire, she could also catch a cold, a cough or runny nose. Then she will die and we don't want that to happen. We want her to remain alive and in good health for a long time. She took care of us for many years. Now we will return what she did for us."

I remember taking care of my grandmother in this way until she died.

Consider the old people:

1. What do you think about the way the Sougb treat their old people?
2. What advice did Dessy's mother give her for taking care of her grandmother?
3. How do people care for the elderly in the West?
4. Discuss the difference between the Sougb people when they no longer work and our old people when they retire?

Folktales

33. *Folktales were told in our houses at night around our home fires. They are called folktales because parts of the story are true and other parts are made up. Each family-clan recited them in a certain way, but the main events and characters are alike. The grandfathers told many stories about our first ancestor, Igba. They repeated them until the next generations knew them by heart. I do not know who wrote these stories down, but it was someone in the very first reading and writing class. —Dessy*

Igba Had Two Wives
Author Unknown

Part One: Igba's Two Wives Have Babies

When Grandfather Igba was a young man he had two wives, Dou-mo-no and Doug-do-ho. They each had a child at the same time in the little birthing house that Igba built beside the big house where they lived. One of the babies was a boy, the other was a girl. The little girl's name was Dou-an-si-ba. The boy's name was Bay-say-g-ba.

Since Igba was the very first ancestor, there was no one else to help his wives. So he went to the garden and got sweet potatoes and firewood for them every day. This was something strange for Igba to do. Now the Sougb men do not go near the birthing hut. It is only the women who help each other.

Igba's wives stayed in the *tu mo-gu-ray* (little house), for a great many months. One day Igba had had enough and told his wives, "You two women, come out right now because your children are already grown."

But Doumono and Dougdoho answered him back, chanting like this:

> *We are sisters like Doumono, bread fruit-o...*
>
> *Dougdoho, bread fruit-o.*
>
> *These babies are our firstborn-o...*
>
> *our very first born-o.*

Igba kept after his wives. But they wouldn't listen. They just sang back to him, repeating the same thing as before:

> *We are sisters like Doumono...*
> *Dougdoho-o.*
> *Like these are our first born-o...*
> *our very first born-o.*

Igba continued bringing food to the little house until his fingernails were worn down. He got very tired digging in the garden and hunting their food. He begged his wives every day to come out, but they refused.

After a long time, he made himself a dugout canoe at the river bank. When it was finished, he called to his wives telling them, "That is all. You two women, come out now!"

But again, they refused to obey their husband's voice. So Igba shot a Bird-of-Paradise and mounted the golden feathers on the front of his new dugout canoe. He paddled down river until he reached the town by the seashore. There he traded the valuable feathers from the Bird-of-Paradise for dowry cloth and seeds for his garden.

After he was gone, Igba's wives got scared and came out of their little hut. They took the two children and looked for him, but they couldn't find him. They cried continually, mourning for him. But it was *jam e-dreg-o-hob,* the hour was already past. It was too late.

Part Two: The Wives Meet In-yom-som-hwa

When Igba went away in the canoe, Doumono and Dougdoho searched for him beside the river and in the rain forest. Along the way, they saw a man-creature. He was dumb and blind; his lips did not speak, nor did his eyes see anything. The women stopped and hid behind the trees and watched the man-creature throw tree nuts into the water along the river. Towards evening, he went into a nearby cave. By that time, the children on their backs felt heavy and the women wanted shelter for the night. They quietly collected dry brush and leaves for firewood and fir-tree boughs to use for sleeping beds. They carried them into the cave but they didn't see a snake that was hidden in the leafy branches they gathered.

Inside the cave, Inyom-somhwa was surprised to hear voices of real people. The women went up to him and put their branches for firewood in a pile at his feet. When he took some twigs to throw into the fire, he grabbed the snake, too. He was so startled that he dropped the twigs and the snake at his feet. In that moment, his whole body began to change right before the women's eyes. Yes, it's true, he really changed, just like that.

His lips and nostrils opened. The eyes and ears opened, and his arms and legs shortened. When he looked like a real man, he opened his mouth and spoke in a real voice to the women, saying, "My name is Inyom-somhwa."

Doumono and Dougdoho were amazed that he changed from a creature into a human before their eyes. But since there was no one else to protect them, they decided to stay and work a garden for him.

Inyom-somhwa was grateful to become a real man. He worked hard for many days, cutting down trees and clearing land for a huge garden. He and the women planted kasava, tapioca root, sweet potatoes, squash, corn, and green beans.

As he worked, he was happy and he sang loudly, "

> *You two made it for me-o…*
>
> *You two did it for me-o.*

Inyom-somhwa was happy in his heart. He praised the names of the two women, saying to them, "You two did magic so that I can walk and talk now. I am a real man now."

After that, the three of them planted more gardens and harvested food from all over the land. They gathered food from as far away as the head waters of the river, by the sea.

Part Three: Igba Finds His Children

Then one day, when they were out in the garden, the women looked up and saw their husband Igba coming down the path. Their children saw him too and began crying and wouldn't stop. They knew Igba was their father and they wanted to go to him.

Igba came closer and picked up the little girl in his arms. Then he lifted the boy. The children stopped crying when he picked them up. Igba didn't say a word to the women. He turned his back on them and carried the children off down the trail. He left the women alone with Inyom-somhwa.

The women started weeping and wailing for their children. Calling after Igba, they yelled,

Be sure you give them bananas-o-o...
because they are so little yet-o.
You give the aigba bird to them-o-o...
because they are small-o.
Give them sweet potatoes to eat-o-o...
because they are still so young-o.

Igba heard their cries and called back to them, "You two sound like the voice of a little cricket near the water. But you are not like the bird calling in the jungle."

He carried both children on his back and went away forever. He took his children all the way to the town of the foreigners. Igba's wives were heartbroken because they never saw their children again.

Think about this:
1. What do you think happened to the two wives that Igba left behind?
2. What parts of the story do you think are true? Made up?
3. What do you think Igba's remarks mean?
    "You two sound like the voice of a little cricket near the water.
      But you are not like the bird calling in the jungle."

34. *My mama told me this same story. It is sad, like many of our old tales. Some people think it is all true, but I think it's only a made-up story from the old people. —Dessy*

A Young Man and His Bird
Mama Desijohota Saiba, Sunggwadis Village

Toucan

In this story of long ago, there was a man named Arech-ay-jan, which means growing grass. His friend was a bird named Bo-de-bay-j. The two of them lived in a house with Arech-ayjan's mother. She was already an old woman and not able to take care of herself.

One day when Arech-ayjan was a teenager, he was playing ball with a girl cousin.

They were throwing a round root that was shaped into a ball. Arech-ayjan accidentally hit his cousin on her bare breast. Hitting her like that was forbidden because it was a taboo to touch her on the breast. So his uncle, the girl's father, made the customary arrangements and brought the girl to Arech-ayjan to take for his wife. The girl's name was I-bro-ro.

Arech-ayjan was happy to have Ibroro for his wife. She was a good help to his blind mother

As was the custom, Arech-ayjan needed dowry goods to pay for his new wife. Since none of the relatives lived close by, he had to travel to their lands in order to borrow cloth, beads and shell ornaments. He depended on his relatives to loan him goods to help him get his wife. He ordered his pet bird to stay with his blind mother and take care of both of them.

The two women and the bird stayed at home, hoping that Arech-ayjan would come back soon, but he didn't. He stayed near his relatives trying to borrow the bridal cloth and shell armbands from them.

When he was gone for a long time, Ibroro started crying for him. She was in the house taking care of her mother-in-law all by herself. Nobody helped her to carry firewood, draw water or dig sweet potatoes in the garden.

Both the mother and Ibroro waited for his return. Finally, the old mother-in-law sang to Arech-ayjan's bird friend,

> *Bodebayj-o...*
> *Bodebayj-o.*
> *You go tell Arech-ayjan-o...*
> *go tell Arech-ayjan-o.*
> *Ibroro is crying for you...*
> *she is really crying for you.*

So Bodebayj flew over the mountains and across the land until he found the house where Arech-ayjan was staying. Bodebayj sat near the doorway of the house and sang out,

> *Arech-ayjan-o...*
> *Arech-ayjan-o.*
> *You come away...*
> *you come away-o.*
> *Your wife is crying for you...*
> *she is really crying for you.*

Meanwhile, back at his home, Ibroro's *medoch mo-mo-go*, her heart was broken, and she died. The old, blind mother was left alone. She mourned and cried in despair,

> *What will happen when I hear footsteps...*
> *when I hear footsteps?*
> *What will happen without my daughter-in-law...*
> *without a grandchild?*

Then she called out for her son, begging him to come home,

> *Where have you gone even now-o...*
> *where are you right now-o.*
> *Because your wife died already...*
> *she died already-o.*

After a while her voice carried far away on the wind, until her son heard it and wondered, *Whose voice is this?*

He started to run on his way towards home. About half-way, he stopped and listened, knowing it was his mother's voice coming to him. Finally, he drew near the house and heard his mother sobbing, louder and louder.

> *Now I am alone...*
> *by myself all the time, all alone-o.*

So Arech-ayjan came home to find his mother alone, and his wife dead in the house. Her body already smelled. No one came to help him. He dug a hole and buried Ibroro. He cried and mourned with his mother in their house.

But even though his wife died, he still owed his in-laws the cloth and beads for a bridal payment. Her father and relatives came to him and he paid them a small part of the dowry price. Then they went away and left him alone to cry with his mother.

Arech-ayjan and his old mother mourned and wept continually for his new bride who was already dead.

Consider this story:

1. Why did Arech-ayjan leave his new bride and his old mother?
2. Who was Bodebayj? What part did he play in the story?
3. Do you think it was fair that Arech-ayjan had to pay for his wife, even though she died? Was this fair?

35. *The Sougb people like to hunt. Old Grandfather, Ig-bo-dau Hway-se-na, from my village, told us this story. Remember, it is only a story, although some people believe it is true. —Dessy*

The Hunter and Many Eyes
Igboudau Hweisena, Sururay Village

There was a hunter who liked to hunt animals with his dog in the jungle. He caught furry tree possum and wild pig. One day when he was out in the thick forest, he spied another man-creature following a dog, like he was also hunting something. The creature was tall, with a very large body and had many eyes. The hunter stayed hidden and watched the man with many eyes for some time.

But finally he called out to him, "Hey, you can have this string bag to carry your possums in."

The man, who was called Many Eyes, stopped and received the bag. "You can follow along with me if you want to."

So the hunter went with him. They were silent and did not talk while they hunted possum. Toward evening, Many Eyes went to a big hole covered over with brush. He crawled inside and the hunter and his dog followed him. It was Many Eyes' cave. Each man sat across from each other on opposite sides of the cave, because they didn't trust each other. They slept sitting up against the wall, too.

The fire had gone down and it was dark. During the night, the man heard Many Eyes quietly talking to his eyes, saying things like this,

"Keep watch on that man over there."

"Why are you looking away at the possums?"

"Haven't you eaten possums like them before?"

"We can skin them and eat them in the morning."

As he listened, the hunter's heart shook. He grew afraid of the strange man, because he knew in his heart that Many Eyes was thinking about eating him and his dog. Hunter whispered to his dog, "Can you dig this hard earth?"

The dog understood his master's voice and started to scratch at the ground but it was packed hard. He dug slowly and was able to make a long tunnel before morning. He spoke softly to his master, "Come, feel this. I dug the ground out already."

The hunter crawled into the tunnel-hole and his dog followed. They crawled all the way to the hunter's house where they believed they were safe.

That same morning after the hunter slept awhile, he called his brothers together and told them about Many Eyes. They rushed to pick up their bows and arrows and hunt the man-creature down before he started looking for them. The hunter led them all back to the cave of Many Eyes.

The brothers crawled into the cave and surprised the man-creature. They shot him over and over again. But he had such a huge body that he didn't die right away. Many Eyes tried to fight back, but the brothers had a gun and they shot him. Then, they burned his body and everything around him into ashes.

After they killed Many Eyes, they ran back to the hunter's house. Not long after that, Hunter and his brothers moved far away to another place. They were afraid to live near the cave home of Many Eyes.

Think about this:

1. Can you think of a fairy tale with a giant similar to Many Eyes?
2. Many Eyes was dead. Why do you think the people moved away after Many Eyes was dead?

36. *Are these stories true, or not? The grandfathers say they are true, but I do not always believe everything from the old stories. We Sougb people of West Papua, Indonesia believe that the Anes and the Sony are actual living creatures. We are no longer afraid of the lake, called Anggi Lake, but we still avoid the mountain ponds and go around them when we are walking on the trails. I don't know if Anes is still in the lake, but even now there are reported sightings of the Sony. —Dessy*

Water Creatures

Grandfather Yonaden Ahoren, Kofo Village

Pond, greatly feared because of spirits

Part One: The Anes

From generations past, our grandfathers thought Anes lived in the mountain ponds. The Anes were creatures who slept in the stagnant ponds on the mountains or in the waters of Lake Anggi Giji. Their bodies are shaped like a snake, but they are short. They each have two heads and two hands. They have the power for making thunder and lightning, big rains and earthquakes.

The waters in the mountain pools are stagnant, murky-black, and sometimes with a layer of green on top. The Sougb avoided the dark ponds and walked around them. Even today, we still circle around them.

It was the same with the waters of Anggi Lake, black and cold, with the waves so angry. The Grandfathers were afraid of the Anes in the lake also. They taught their children not to walk close to the lakeshore, but to take the paths higher up above the forests surrounding the lake.

The Grandfathers warned their children, "Stay away from any of the waters where the Anes live."

Part Two: The Sony

The Sony is another creature who lives at waterfalls. They are the guardian of the waters. Their bodies are like a human's, only smaller and their limbs are long. Their fingers, fingernails and teeth are also extra-long. They walk upright like a man and their feet are like ours. But a Sony walks faster than people because his legs and feet are so long. There are boy and girl Sonys.

Nowadays people say that a Sony lives at Unyai by the waters of Sirij, which is a place close to the village of Nenay. Another Sony lives at Wausugb Falls which is near Sohu. Others people report they have seen Sonys at other waterfalls in the Sougb lands too.

Consider the stories:

1. The Sougb people believe the Anes and Sony are real creatures?
   What do you think?
2. If you lived in Sougb-land, would you visit the mountains ponds and waterfalls?
   Why, or why not?

37. *After explaining about the Anes and Sony, Grandfather Yonaden told a true story about a living Sony. I am not sure I believe everything in his story either. But Grandfather Yonaden's relatives say it really happened. -Dessy*

The Creature at the Waterfall
A true story, Grandfather Yonaden Ahoren, Kofo Village

One day my older brother went hunting for jungle hen eggs and left his wife and son at their small house. On his hunt for the eggs, he came to a waterfall and he stopped to look at the mist drifting around behind the falls. Suddenly, he saw a Sony sitting behind the water. He hid himself in the trees and watched. The Sony's body was in shadow behind the falls, but he could see it was shaped like a man, only he had extra-long fingers, nails, and long teeth. My older brother didn't want to show himself to the Sony, so he went on his way.

Later that day the Sony came out from behind the falls. He found his way to my older brother's house in the jungle near the village of Sihu. He saw my brother's wife sitting in the house. He walked right into the jungle house, took her by the hand and led her to the waterfall.

When my older brother came home from hunting, he looked all over for his wife and couldn't find her anywhere. My father was sitting there and he told him, "Your wife was alone in the house, and the Sony came and took her. You go back now and get a gun. Take a shell and powder, and make a bullet to put in the barrel of your gun."

My brother followed his voice and made the bullet from gun powder and loaded it in the gun. Then he asked twelve young men to go with him. When they neared the waterfall, they divided up in order to search at another waterfall nearby. Two of them stayed and hid their bodies at the first waterfall. They discovered two pairs of footprints in the sand. One set was like a real person's, but the other set was like flat footprints. So they knew the woman, my brother's wife, was still there with the Sony.

When they got closer to the falls they saw a cleared space behind the falls. The Sony had opened a door and allowed a woman to sit behind the water on a rock in the sun. She was alone and the Sony was not there. They looked closer and it was really and truly my brother's wife, in the flesh. My brother quietly hid out of sight, and shouldering his gun, he waited for the Sony to come back.

When the Sony returned, he frowned and they heard him grumble to the woman, "Why are you sitting here? You go on inside."

While he was standing there, talking to the woman, her husband fired the gun and shot him. The Sony fell back through the waterfall, into the deep water. He disappeared from sight.

My brother waited and when he saw that the Sony was truly gone, he took his wife's hand and brought her back safely to their jungle house. Not long after that, they burned their house down and everyone moved away from the waterfall. They were afraid to live in that place.

What do you think about this story?

1. Why do you think the wife went with the Sony?
2. What do you think really happened to the Sony when they shot him?
3. Would you have moved after the Sony was shot?

38. *This is one of the stories from my ancestors that my grandmother told me. —*
Dessy

How the Trees Were Named
Mama Desijohota Saiba, Sunggwadis Village

Tribal village along the seashore

This story is about a boy snake called Linya and a girl snake named Suwu.
already

One day Linya went to a waterhole named Merugwaha where the snakes were
cooking food for a feast. Linya had many older brothers and sisters who were
gathered there. One older brother they called Snago, another was named Skougwa,
one was called Mihiga, and the youngest sister was named Dago. They all ate
together. When their feasting was over, they danced all night.

At the dance, the girl snake Suwu sat by the side of the waterhole. She saw Linya and she really liked him. He also liked her and wanted her for his wife. Everyone danced all night until daylight. Suwu waited until dawn and then she followed Linya. They left quietly and went to a mountain close by.

Linya's brothers and sisters continued their feasting and dancing by the waterhole for several more days. They looked around for Linya and Suwu, but didn't see them. They made up a song about them.

> *Suwu, Linya...*
> *Suwu, Linya.*
> *You tricked us...*
> *you went out away from us.*
> *You fooled us...*
> *you went out and left us.*

The brothers and sisters did not go out searching for them, because they were not worried about them. Besides, they wanted to stay at the waterhole and party.

—*In these days, we took the names of the snakes for our trees. We call them the snago tree, the skougwa tree, and the me-hi-ga tree. But the name dahgo, we Sougb, we only say ah-go, and that is what we call our g-string to hold the loincloth on.* —*Dessy*

Consider this story:

1. What kind of story is this?
2. Do you think this is a true story? Partly true? Which part?

The Sougb People Follow Jesus Path

Church leaders gathered for preaching lessons

39. When missionaries first came to tell the Sougb tribe about the true God, Jesus the Son, and the Pure Spirit, my people still followed the old paths of fighting with each other and killing their enemies with sorcery and witchcraft. They didn't know anything about the God who created the world and loved them. For seven years they listened to Bible stories and preaching from the whiteskins, or we also called them foreigners. Finally, Grandfather Yonaden and several other men told the missionary they were ready to follow Jesus' path. This is Grandfather Yonaden's story. —Dessy

My Life When I Followed Jesus
Pastor Yonaden Ahoren - Kofo Village

When I was a young man, I lived with my family in a town along the coast of this island. At that time, the Dutch ruled our land and everyone spoke the Malay language in public. But at home, we only talked in the Sougb language. We were wicked people, practicing witchcraft to kill our enemies. We didn't understand about a God who made us and loved us.

In the town by the sea, the Dutch foreigners had a church. I decided to take my family to hear what they had to say. After we attended many times, the pastor put drops of water on our foreheads and gave us each a Christian name. Then he told us that now we could enter heaven, because we were baptized and had new names. I believed what he said was true, and I thought I was a Christian.

—But in my heart, everything was the same.

—I still liked women; it was the same.

—I used black magic against my enemies; it was the same.

—I really liked doing bad things; it was the same.

—Inside myself, my *heart was always hot*, I did mean things to other people.

Then one day I took my family and moved back to the mountains by a big lake. A Dutch teacher lived in my village then and he taught school in the Malay language. On Sundays, he told Bible stories about God and Jesus. He never showed us anything about our sin. He said that we were all good. Again, nothing changed in my life.

Later, other *whiteskins,* missionaries, came from America to live with us. They held meetings on the grass airstrip on Sunday afternoons. They learned to talk our Sougb voice and translated Bible stories for us. They did not always say the words correctly and they spoke very slowly, but I could understand them. And when I heard the stories about Jesus in my own tongue, they *hit my heart* every time.

After a while, the missionary asked me to go with him in his aluminum row boat to villages around the lake. The people gathered together in each of these places and he told them the stories about Jesus. We went out like this for three days each week.

One Sunday morning at my village, the missionary asked me to pray. My *heart really shook,* "Oh, no, my heart is scared. What can I say? I don't know how to pray yet."

But the missionary encouraged me, "Don't be afraid. I will go ahead of you, just follow my voice, like this:

> *Jesus, God, I hear your voice.*
> *And I want to follow you.*
> *I open the door to my heart and show you my sin.*
> *Wash away my sin and I will turn away from it, too.*
> *Enter my heart now and sit next to me.*
> *You will eat with me. I will eat with you.*
> *—Amin*

I prayed that prayer with my voice shaking, because I did not understand it all in my heart yet. But I knew that God was speaking to *my innermost,* and I wanted to follow Jesus.

After he brought me to Jesus, the missionary asked me to go to church with him and help explain his words. We started the first church in my village, and I was chosen to be a pastor. We called ourselves Shepherds. At that time also, I began to help the missionary in his office with our language, and he wrote it all down on paper. I worked with him all the time after that.

Bringing items of witchcraft and sorcery to burn

Think about these things:

1. Was anything different after the Dutch pastor put water on Yonaden's forehead?

2. Why was it easier for him to follow the missionary's prayer?

3. How did he help the missionary?

Special terms, what do you think they mean?

Pure Spirit	*whiteskins*
my heart was always hot	*my innermost*
Shepherd	*my heart shook*
sits next to me	*You will eat with me, I will eat with you*

40. When Pastor Yonaden prayed with the missionary, he didn't know very much about God. But he decided to stay on Jesus' path and not live with a wicked heart anymore. The Holy Spirit helped him to know that Jesus was real and this was the right path to follow. —Dessy

The Holy Spirit Gives Yonaden a Sign
Pastor Yonaden Ahoren, Kofo Village

A few days after I asked Jesus into *my innermost place*, my heart, I went on a raft across the big lake to another village. I traveled there to get a pig that a man promised me. A friend went with me and we tied the pig's legs together with vine and put it on the raft to paddle back across the lake.

It was daytime, but dark and cloudy. In the middle of the lake I saw a big star shining very brightly. It dropped from heaven below the clouds, like a bamboo torch falling from the sky. The light around the star broke into streams of different colors: white, red, yellow, green and blue. We were in great awe and wonder and thought to ourselves, "What can this be? Is it from lightning?" We were so amazed we could not speak.

When I saw the light in the sky, I heard the Pure Holy Spirit speak to my heart. I knew the burning torch was a sign to me about doing bad things, like using sorcery and black magic. The White Spirit reminded me about the black magic poison I kept in secret to put the hex on the people I thought had killed my father. I wanted to use it to get revenge and pay them back. I had the poison stored in a hollow bamboo tube and hid it in my house, away from the eyes of my wife and children.

I was thinking about this, and then I remembered. I already prayed with the Missionary a few days before going across the lake. At that time, I *opened my heart*, and told Jesus about my sins. That meant I was already walking on Jesus path now. The Holy Spirit was telling me not to use sorcery anymore. Immediately, I knew that I must go home and get the poison out of my house. I had to throw it away from me.

My friend and I rowed the rest of the way to my village. He took care of the pig while I went up the notched pole into my house. I gathered my family around me and gave this witness to them:

"Three days ago, I prayed with the missionary to ask Jesus to enter my heart. I *revealed all of my sins* to God and now *he sits next to me.*

Today, when we were on the lake, I saw a bright light coming down from heaven, like a bamboo torch, a star. It was a sign from God to show me He is the real, true God. The Pure Holy Spirit was also showing me I must not practice witchcraft anymore, because it is a path that leads to wickedness. Now, I want to take all my black magic bags and poisons and not use them ever again."

I went to my hiding place and showed the poisons to my family and relatives, so they could be my witnesses. "This poison was for me to hex people and avenge my father's death. Until now my heart was filled with *thorns of evil.* Today, I want all of you to look at the poison, because now I am getting rid of it. The Holy Spirit is my guide now, and He is showing me my sin. Therefore, I'm going to toss all of it back to the spirits in the lake forever."

When I saw the lights on the lake and listened to the Pure Spirit speak to my heart, I knew God was real, and his Spirit is with me and will teach me what is right. This is true, and I ask God's Spirit to direct me for the rest of my life.

Think about Pastor Yonaden's story:
1. Tell about his vision?
2. What did he think it meant? Do you agree?
3. Why did he have poison hidden in his house?
4. Why did he show the poison to the people in his house?
5. Terms and their meaning:

   opened my heart

   revealed all of my sins

   thorns of evil
6. What are other names for the Holy Spirit from the story?
7. What is a miracle? Do you think this story tells about one?

41. *I was a little girl when the missionaries came to our land. I don't know the exact date, because we did not use calendars then. I only know I was old enough to help my mother in the garden and take care of my younger sister and brother. Every Sunday the white-skins invited us to come to the grass airstrip near their houses to hear Bible stories. This is my story about going around the lake with the missionaries to other villages. —Dessy*

Telling About Jesus
Dessy Saiba, Sunggwadis village

Telling a Bible picture story

When I was a little girl, I didn't follow Jesus yet. We had a Dutch teacher in my village, and he taught grades 1-6 in the government school. On Sunday he told us Bible stories in the Malay language. I listened, but I couldn't understand him. Only the missionaries, the *whiteskins, tried* to learn our Sougb voice. Every day they told us Bible stories. They talked slowly, but I was happy because I could understand what they said.

They also showed us Bible pictures with each story. I asked to take the pictures home with me to tell the stories to my family. I remember the first picture was Adam and Eve in the Garden of Eden. I took many picture stories home with me, and my father allowed me to sit by his fire every night and tell the stories to anyone who would listen. I told them over and over. For myself, when I heard the stories, they *sat in my heart* for a long time. I liked them, but I wasn't ready to believe they were true.

One day, the missionary ladies invited me and two of my friends to go with them around the lake to another village. They wanted to show the Bible story pictures and tell the stories there. They also took medicine to give to those who were sick. That first time, we stayed all day and night in a village without eating. The people couldn't give us anything because their gardens were empty. We slept at my uncle's house and came home the next morning, very hungry. After that, I went out to other villages and heard the missionaries tell the stories many times. We took our own food or ate at someone's house in those places. All that time, I still didn't really know Jesus yet, but I was thinking about everything they were teaching.

The Book of Colors

On another Sunday at the airstrip, the missionary showed us a little book with only colored pages, no words. He gave me one to take home to show my mother and father. The *Book of Colors* had special meaning:

> **Black page**—to tell us we all have sinned.
> **Red page**—is for Jesus' blood that covered our sin.
> **White page**—our hearts are washed clean when we
> tell Jesus our sins
> **Green page**, **Blue page**, and **Yellow pages**—show us the
> path that leads to heaven.

I told many in my family and my village about the *Book of Colors* and how Jesus died for our sins. This is what I said, but I didn't believe it in my heart yet.

The Voice Machine

Then there was the *foreign voice machine*. It was like a little black box with a hand-crank and it played Bible stories in our Sougb tongue. When I heard the stories and words from this machine, the words *hit my heart,* and I wanted to follow Jesus. My father and mother liked to listen to it also, but they did not want to follow Jesus. Later, I was allowed to carry the voice machine and the *Book of Colors* in my string bag and show them to my relatives over the mountain. Some of them chose to follow Jesus when they heard the stories and understood about the colors. I explained and taught them all that I knew about Jesus.

When I was about ten years old, I was ready to believe all about Jesus and that he died for me and my sins on the cross. I went with my cousin Me-reej to talk to our pastor, because we both wanted to enter the baptismal class so that we could be counted as Christians. We prayed with Pastor Yonaden and *revealed all that was in our hearts* to God. We asked Jesus into our hearts. Pastor Yonaden put our names on the list for baptismal classes.

A sign for Dessy

Not long after starting the baptismal class, God showed me how he loves and takes care of us. My sister and I were hunting in the forest and our dog chased a possum. We shot the possum with an arrow. When we brought it back to our camp, our fire near the stream was in ashes, and we did not have any more fire sticks to start a new fire and cook the possum. I prayed and asked God to help me. Then I searched in the ashes and found a glowing ember underneath everything. I gathered dry grasses and put them in the ashes and blew on them. Our fire started and we cooked our supper. This is how God took care of us when I prayed.

Think about these things:

1. In what ways did Dessy and the missionaries share the Bible stories?
2. Explain the meaning of the colors in the Book of Colors.
3. Why do you think Dessy kept telling the Bible stories even though she didn't believe them?
3. Terms and their meaning:

white-skins   *sat in my heart*

foreign voice machine   *words hit my heart*

       revealed all that was in our hearts

42. *Big changes came to my people when they decided to follow Jesus' path. For generations, they had walked their own trails and now the elders were discussing whether to accept a new way, a path that no one had ever taken before. There were only eight people, seven men and one woman, who dared to go to the missionary. He prayed with them and they opened their hearts to God. Those eight entered the first of many baptismal classes to learn Bible verses and receive instruction about how to live in God's way. When the lessons were completed, they were baptized in Anggi Lake. This lesson tells about the beginning classes when only a few wanted to follow Jesus. —Dessy*

Baptismal Class

Baptism in the jungle

The Missionary taught us from the *Letter of Dunking Under the Water*. First, he translated everything into the Sougb voice. These verses and the lessons showed us about following God, Jesus Christ and the Holy Spirit.

Pastor Yonaden told about his first class. *The Letter of Dunking Under the Water* told us like this:

> *Why are you being dunked under the water?*
> *I answered it was because I wanted to follow*
> *God's voice. Therefore, I revealed my sins,*

named them to God. and became his child.

Mama Dessy-jo-ho-ta also told about her baptismal class, "When I opened up my sins and told them to God, Pastor Yonaden was the one who prayed with me and brought me to Jesus. After I studied the lessons and Bible verses in class, he asked me like this:

Do you still go to the village dances?

I said I turned away from that.

Do you eat the pig's spirit now?

I turned away from that.

Do you smoke the weed (marijuana) from the mountains?

I never did that.

How many days will you follow Jesus path?

I will follow this path for many days,

all the years of my life, until Jesus comes, or I die.

My life was changed and I knew that Jesus was real and He loved me.

Questions to think about:

1. What do you think eating the pig's spirit means, smoking the weed?
2. Why would the pastor ask questions like that?
3. Terms and their meaning:

    Letter of Dunking Under the Water

    opened up my heart, revealed my sins

    follow God's voice
4. What does *opened up my heart* mean to you?

43. It took over 23 years for Missionary Lunow to finish translating the Sougb New Testament. When it was ready to be sent to the printer, we had a big celebration in our church. Pastor Yonaden, our first pastor, was still living and he prepared a letter to read to the missionaries at that service. They were surprised by the letter, and we all cried together. It was the first time the Sougb people said "thank you" to our missionaries. —Dessy

A Thank You Letter from the Sougb Church

First Sougb Church Leaders

This letter is to our missionaries, whose names we lift up. I, Shepherd Yonaden, am giving you our voice from the Sougb Church:

We heard that you finished translating the Letter of God's Voice to us. First of all, we thank God, because His heart turned towards us. Therefore, He sent you missionaries to bring the message of Jesus' word. Now you have changed God's voice into our voice for all of the Sougb people. You did this for us, because we were all in darkness forever.

Indeed, right now, we thank you because you brought your light to shine on our land. You showed us the path to enter this light also. God has raised up many people as His blood drops, His true adopted children, because you brought Jesus to us.

We also thank you many times, because you are using up your energy and efforts to nurture and take care of us by teaching God's word, which is good, always. And your conduct is consistent with the message of God's word that you are bringing us, most certainly this is true.

With this letter, we are giving you our dowry-bead necklace of thanks. They are worth very little because they are from this earth. But what you brought us is beyond price in Heaven. All our bridal cloth and bead necklaces, their cost does not nearly approach the worth of God's Word, which keeps gaining in value. So whatever we give back to you is only measured by value on this earth. But that which is much more costly and permanent, God will give to you as your reward in heaven for bringing us Jesus.

This is all. May God protect you on the pathway. May He continue to give you wisdom as you take our Sougb Voice to be printed into a book, the Sougb Bible.

God keep you until we meet again.

May-jee-ray-so, your life to you.

Shepherd Yonaden and the Anggi Church.

New Testament presented to Pastor Banner Yonaden

God Speaks Now in Our Own Tongue

New Testaments shown by the Taigeh Church

Reading the Sough New Testament by the Fireside

Questions to consider:

1. What terms can you find that are used for the word, 'language'?

2. What do you think *his heart turns towards us* means?

3. What light did the missionaries bring to the Sougb people?

4. Why do the Sougb people say what the missionary brings is *beyond price and it keeps gaining in value*?

44. After the Sougb New Testament was translated and published, God showed us that other tribes had not yet heard about God's love for them. Pastor Urias, who was on the translation team for the New Testament, and his wife, Lois, were the first couple sent out by the Sougb Church to tell others this good news. Today there are ten Sougb families sent out to other tribes as missionaries.   —Dessy

The First Sougb Missionary Family

First Sougb missionary family

Grandfather, Pastor Yonaden spoke like this, saying to us all,

"We Sougb men are like the trees that stand still where their roots are planted. We stay in our home plots, like our grandfathers and fathers did before us. But our daughters are like the moss on a tree. They go out from our homes to another tree. They go to their husband's birth-land.

Today is a new day for the Sougb church. My son-in-law, Urias, is going away from us, like the moss on a tree. He will go away from his own family to another place. He does this, because he wants to follow God's direction and whatever the Holy Spirit tells him to do. He is going away from the tree on his birth-land to foreign soil, so that he, and his wife Lois and their children, can show Jesus to the people there.

Therefore, may God give them good things, placing his many blessings on them. I ask that God go before them and behind them, as they leave for this faraway place, a place they do not know. Urias is leading his family to a strange people, a people who speak a new voice, a language they do not yet understand.

This is my own daughter, Lois, who is going with her husband to a foreign place, where she will be a helper to him. Together they will bring the story of Jesus love to ones who have never heard about him. May they go in God's strength. Amin"

Questions:

1. How are Sougb husbands described by Pastor Yonaden?
2. How are Sougb wives described?
3. What is the meaning of *his heart turned towards us*?
4. What is the light that missionaries bring?
5. Why did Urias and Lois leave their birth-land?
   Do you think it was easy for them?

45. In this last story, I invite you to come to Papua, Indonesia through the eyes of your imagination. Although the story is fiction, the thoughts and expressions were shared with me from several of my Sougb friends.

Now, picture yourself sitting with your feet stretched out to the log fire in a bark hut on a dark, misty mountain. Take a deep breath and smell the wood smoke. Relax, rest.

It's the first time you've held a book in your hands. And it's in your own language; you can understand what it says. Let yourself FEEL what the coming of the Voice of God (the Bible) means to a tribal people.

Listen from your heart as a young tribal girl tells her story; like it was yesterday, like it is today, like she believes it will be tomorrow, since God's voice came to her people.

—-Barbara Lunow, author

Yesterday, Today, Tomorrow

Long ago, in the days of our grandfathers, the fires glowed and crackled nightly in our bark houses perched on the mountain slopes of the rain forests. In those hours, while sitting in the shadows of the firelight, our grandfathers told stories of fleeing to the highlands from slave traders. They repeated the legend of a giant whose footprints, in the beginning of time, formed male and female lakes which they feared in the valleys below.

Speaking in our own Sougb voice, the fathers whispered to their sons the secrets of sorcery and witchcraft. They passed down their powers of manipulation and control over the spirits that daily threatened their lives. These were the very spirits who caused them to always live in constant fear and dread.

Every evening, Sun slid behind the mountains into darkness, while inside their bark houses the wood fires burned and crackled with light and warmth. As the night hours wore on the flames died down into glowing embers, then smoldering ashes. Every morning Sun threw his feet over the mountain ridges, stretching them out into warm rays. This is how it was in the grandfathers' time, when many people lived, and many died. This was the way it happened, most certainly.

Then one day when my mother was a child, like me, strangers came to live close to Boy Lake down in the valley. My mother wanted to see them and so she took skin, gathered courage, and walked down the mountain path to the tin house where the white-skinned people told stories—ones that the Sougb had never heard before. These foreigners gave my mother a small *Book of Colors*, which she tucked away in her little string bag to carry back home. The book had no written words in it, only colored pages. In the time before now, writing did not matter because none of my people knew letters on paper yet.

That very night Grandfather allowed my mother to sit by his fire while she told the story of the *Book of Colors*. The first page, a black page, was like the deep, dark waters of Male Lake. A red page was the color of the feet of Sun reaching over the mountains into the morning. White page looked like clouds in the sky. Green page was the same color as the dense lowland jungles. Blue looked like the heavens above. Gold page was like corn ripened and ready to eat. They were colors my mother knew and understood very well.

But listen, the strangers said the story of the *Book of Colors* had another meaning also. The black page showed the darkness which separates all of mankind from the true God, because our inner thoughts and outward actions are unclean before the One who is a Pure Spirit. Red was for the blood of someone called Jesus, who died on a cross to cover over the blackness of our hearts. White showed how we can be washed and made clean inside when we reveal our sins to God and turn away from them. Then we can *sit next to this Jesus*, who is God's son.

My mother couldn't tell all of it rightly, because the story was new and some things were strange to her and hard to understand. None of her many relatives had ever heard the story of colors before either. She wanted to keep going to hear the slow words of the strangers who were learning to speak our language and put the sounds and letters on paper. They told about a God whose name is not only over all, but He also loves all people. My mother listened carefully so she could remember the picture-stories they gave her and tell them at home.

Night upon night, in the smoky, gray darkness, she sat by her father's fireside and told any who would listen about her picture-stories. Her *eyes were blind to the words* written down, but she clearly remembered every story and every picture. She told them over and over again.

Today

In my days now, as I am growing up, my mother still tells her stories to me and my sister and brothers. She *gives her voice* to us, like this, "When I hear God's letter read in our Sougb voice, I can understand it. I know it is right, because it speaks to *my innermost* and gives me peace. The words tell me to follow after the true God. They urge me to *take the path after his only son Jesus*, who died on a cross for me. I know this great God loves us women, in the same way He loves the men. His voice teaches us that we have souls, we can think, we can learn. We don't have to be afraid of all the taboos concerning us and our children anymore. Surely this is right; God's words are true and trustworthy."

In this present time, when Sun's feet appear over the mountains, I take my big string bag and go to the gardens to plant and dig sweet potatoes with my mother, the same as my grandmothers did before me. At nightfall we bring home our potatoes and vegetables, fresh drinking water from the spring, and bundles of firewood. This is how our daily lives have been since the days of the Grandfathers.

But now there is more! I am learning to read and write God's message to us in my own tongue, the Sougb voice. The true God has given me a mind for these things. My eyes not only see it on paper, but I understand what it means in my head, and I place it close in my heart. Now I, too, trust Jesus and sit next Him. All of this is true, yes, indeed it is.

There is also the one special morning, when Sun awakens and spreads warmth over the mountains into a new week. That day we don't go to the gardens. Early in the morning we wash in the cold stream, and when the conch shell blows we go down the trail to *God's Sunday House*. There, we chant verses and pray. The *shepherd*, pastor, reads and preaches the message of God to us, explaining it in words and stories that we can understand.

Our shepherd is an old man but he speaks in a strong voice, "Listen, to what I say. When I was a young man, I used to carry my amulets, charms and black magic things in my little net bag under my arm, just as my fathers did before me. I trusted in these things for protection, for scaring away spirits, and for putting the hex on my enemies. But now, I stand on the choice I made long ago, to follow Jesus' path only. My heart is set firm upon everything that I read from God's book; that it is all true, forever. Today, I still carry in my string bag the thing I trust in above everything else. It is the book of *God's New Promise*, the Bible. I urge you all, every one of you, whatever you hear right now in the preaching of this book that is true and right, take it and put it in your own string bag and carry it with you, always."

Tomorrow

So it is, in the evenings now, as Sun slides behind the ranges, leaving the heavens gray and dark, the fires still glow and burn in our bark houses on the mountains and in the valley near Male Lake. My father no longer passes down the secrets of sorcery in the shadows of night. Instead, he leads us as we clap our hands and chant our verses, and *lift up God's name*—the name that is over all. God's Pure Spirit frees us from the fears of the spirit-world we live in. We praise him for the peace that he gives us in our hearts, for the love he gives us for our enemies.

We all, my sister and I, and my father and brothers too, sit stretching our feet to the fire. My mother smiles and tells again, the story of the coming of the whiteskins, our missionaries, who *opened the door* for us to know about the God who made everything, and about Jesus, His son.

Hear my voice now, all of you, because I am telling you this with a happy heart. Nightly, when I sit by the firelight, I hold in my hands a real book, written in our Sougb voice, the voice that we understand. I read the book of *God's New Promise* out-loud to all of my family whose eyes are still blind to the words. Then we talk about God's message that is written in our own language and speaks truth to our hearts.

This is how it is in my days, already. And so it will be tomorrow, and in all the days to follow, when Sun's glow slips away over the mountains, and my children and grandchildren sit by their fires in the bark houses of the Sougb people.

And I pray, "Yoh, dear daddy God, in Heaven: let it be so, now and forever, always, Amin."

Glossary of Sougb Terms:

A

abaga (a-ba-ga) —white, round, shell armband

Ahoren (A-ho-ren) —clan name

Aigba (Eye-g-ba) -first ancestor of the Sougb people; also name of a certain bird

aigdaga (eye-g-da-ga) — vines, used to tie houses together

amplok (am-plok) —icicle shaped shell body decoration

ampoun (am-po-un) —glass trade beads used for dowry payment

Anes (A-nes) —a spirit with a physical body that lived in Anggi Giji

Anggi Gida (Ang-gee Gee-da) — Girl Lake

Anggi Giji (Gee-jee) —Boy Lake

ansee (an-see) —dark, stagnant pools found on the mountain tops

Anuk (A-nook) —a garden location behind Sururay village

Arech-ayjan (Ar-ech-ay-jan) —a man's name, means 'growing grass'

B

ban abdoc an len (ban ab-doch an len) -turn your heart towards them

ban bemedreg ban abina men gesedougwo dara en mer (ban be-me-dreg ban a-bi-na men ge-se-dou-gwo en mer) —do not step outside of your father's care and advice.

ban besedougwo ban absira (ban be-se-dou-gwo ban ab-si-ra) —keep your hands off

ban besedougwo ban abiresi (ban be-se-dou-gwo ban a-bi-re-see) —guard your eyes

ban bowun ban abdoch mes, besedougwo ban abtemouwu (ban bo-wun ban ab-doch mes, be-se-dou-gwo ban ab-te-mou-woo), lower your heart and keep your tongue

ban abdoch etrij icira (ban ab-doch- e-treej ee-ci-ra) -your heart flutters over, covets

ban augwan, dan augwan (ban auw-gwan, dan auw-gwan) —all of you, all of me

ban besedougwo ban abaga (ban be-se-dou-gwo ban a-ba-ga), always guard your body

Baraymer (Ba-ray-mer) —son of Sogora and Dayagaris

Bapak (Ba-pak) —mister, sir, term of respect, Indonesian word

Baysaygba (Bay-sayg-ba) —boy's name, son of Aigba

besara-bohwara (be-sa-ra bo-hwa-ra), to work diligently and be generous

Bodebayj (Bo-de-bayj) —bird friend of Arechayjan

bogo erechiraha (bo-go er-e-chi-ra-ha) —the heaven (sky) shows a crack of light on the horizon between the darkness, about 4AM

bogo obrurugb (bo-go o-brew-rew-gb) -early morning heavens break up, rays of the sun shine through, about 5AM

Bomjohw (Bom-johw) —people from the island of Timor

booch —to pass gas

Buchgemehir (Buch-ge-me-hir) -first man who discovered Anggi Lakes

buch mandeich (buch man-deich) —the main, center pole to a house

C

chinchokobed (chin-cho-ko-bed) —hiccup

chugwemera (choo-gwe-me-ra) —faded red, round, large glass bead

D

Dago (Da-go) —name of snake

Dayagaris (Day-a-ga-rees) —wife of Sogora from the Saiba clan, she had skin disease

Desingmay (De-sing-may) —woman Domstera village

Dibetig (Di-be-tic) —mountain village where Sougb hid from soldiers

Dirirbo (Deer-eer-bo) —name of a mountain

Disihu (Di-see-hoo) —village on Anggi Lake

Dobmoro (Dob-mo-ro) —woman's name

Douansiba (Dou-an-see-ba) -girl's name, daughter of Aigba; a clan name

Dougdoho (Doug-do-ho) —girl's name, wife of Aigba

Doumono (Do-mo-no) —girl's name, wife of Aigba

E

echee (e-chee) —sneeze

echingga (e-ching-ga) —belch

eenyoomda (een-yoom-da) — earthquake rumble

eigtou desij (egg-tow de-seej) —sit next to, stay with

eija (ay-ja) —shake, shiver

ekris (e-krees) —fold, braid hair

G

gohob (go-hob) —foundation poles

gowi (go-wee) —-name of tree, used to make rafts

Grandfather Kubay (Koo-bay) —oldest man in Sunggwadis village

H

hirog, clay fireplaces in houses

hom   — one, 1; the right hand grasps the left thumb

hwai —two, 2; the right hand grasps thumb and forefinger

homoy (ho-moy) —three, 3; the right hand " 	" " two fingers

hogu (ho-gu) —four,4; " 	" " " " " three fingers

Hosma   —village beyond the lakes

I

Ibroro (Ee-bro-ro) —wife of Arecheijan

Ibu (Ee-boo)   —Mrs., mama, term of respect, Indonesian word

Igba (Eeg-ba) — first Sougb ancestor, man's name, lan name

Igbodau Hwaysena (Eeg-bo-dau Hway-se-na) —man's name

igdabogo (ig-da-bo-go) —the sun touches the heavens, 11-12 Noon

igda edeij (ig-da e-day-j) —the sun is bending over, 3-4 PM

igda ehin maga (ig-da e-heen ma-ga) —the sun turns his body sideways, 1-2 PM

igda erba mohora (ig-da er-ba mo-ho-ra) —the sun throws out his feet

igda obsaresohob, (ig-da ob-sa-re-so-hob) —the sun fell already; sunset, 6-7 PM

ig-dech-gwa -notched pole up to house

igdes ohu deslougb ((ig-des o-hoo des-lougb) —the sun gives, brings heat, 8-10 AM

Ijom (Ee-jom) —Hatam tribal name

Ijom-medigo (Ee-jom-Med-I-go) —man from Inyomusi clan

Ijommur (Ee-jom-mur) —village name

Ihwayj (Ee-hway-j) —man's name

Imchin (Eem-cheen) —tribal name

Indou (In-dou) —family, clan name

Inyom-somhwa (Een-yom-som-hwa) —man's name

inyomstega (een-yom-ste-ga) —hollow burial tree at Anuk, near Sururay village

Inyuhumei (Een-yu-hu-may) —location in the mountains

Inyomusi (Een-yo-mu-see) —clan, family name

J

jam edregohob (jum e-dreg-o-hob) —the hour is already past

K

Kain Timor (Keye-n Tee, mor) —special woven cloth from island of Timor

L

libogo (lee-bo-go) = rare, darker blue, small, round glass bead

limogo gogoufu (lee-mo-go go-go-foo) = common, white beads

limaga merij (me-reej) = common, smaller, light yellow bead

limogo (lee-mo-go) —common glass beads

limaga (lee-ma-ga) —light yellow glass bead

limayj (lee-may-j) —darker yellow glass bead

liampoum (lee-am-pom) —large, blue glass bead

Linya (Leen-ya) —snake's name

lonamenmen (lo-na-men-men) —the light of day, it comes, it comes

losog (lo-sog) —5-6 PM, the sun is falling behind the horizon

lomuchmuch (lo-mooch-mooch) —light and darkness meet together

lobayngmod (lo-bay-ng-mod) —12 MN, the moon closes over the sky

Louwi (Lo-wee) —tribal name

lusud mos (lu-sud moss) —adult or mature, skin

M

Makasa (Ma-ka-sa) —unknown land where the foreigners came from

Manden (Mahn-den) —location in the lowlands

Manokwari (Ma-no-kwa-ree) —coastal town where Sougb traded

Manugwo (Ma-nu-gwo) —man's name

Meijireso (may-jee-re-so) -greeting, hello and goodbye, meaning: your life to you

mem prau —cheap, red and yellow beads

Merugwaha (Me-ru-gwa-ha) —a waterhole where the snakes gathered

mesira hwai (me-si-ra hwai) — two hands; ten

mesira hwai, mohora hom (me-si-ra hom) —fifteen; two hands, one foot

mesira hwai, mohora hwai —twenty; two hands, two feet

minch menau (minch me-nau,) — new woven cloth, used for dowry

Mihiga (Mee-hee-ga) —-name of snake

Momi (Mo-mee) —town in the district of Manokwari

Mindiri (min-deer- ree) —spirits, ghosts of the dead

mok-mok —bad, evil, fearsome

moleich (mo-lay-ch) -name of a tree

N

Nenay (Ne-nay) —village, mission station

Nona (no-na) —Miss, term of respect, Indonesian word

Nyonya (Nyo-nya) —Mrs., missus, term of respect, Indonesian word

O

os maga (os ma-ga) —hang on to a body

R

Ransiki (Ran-see-kee) —coastal town

S

Saiba (Seye-ba) —clan, family name

sariou (sa-ree-o) —rare pearls, or white glass beads with cloisonné design

Satobmod (Sa-tob-mod) —location in the lowlands

Saugwa (sau-gwa) name of snake, name of tree

      Sirga (seer-ga), name of snake, name of tree

      Skougwa (Skou-gwa) —name of snake, name of tree

      Snago (sna-go) —name of snake, name of tree

      Steiga (stay-ga), —name of snake, name of tree

sergem (ser-gem) —five, 5; all left hand fingers, or one hand

senggem (seng-gem) —six, 6; the left hand grasps the right thumb

senggai (seng-gai) —seven, 7; the left hand   "   "   "   "   and forefinger

senggemoy (seng-ge-moy) —eight, 8; "   "   "   "   "   "   two fingers

senggegu (seng-ge-goo) —nine, 9; "   "   "   "   "   "   three fingers

sibeej (si-beej)— tree bark used for flooring and outside of new house

Sigbayna (Seeg-bay-na) —tribal group

Sihu (See-hoo) —village near Nenay

Sijeray (See-je-ray) —man's name

Sinsinemes (Sin-sin-e-mes) —name of a mountain

Sirij (Si-reej) —location close to Nenay

Sisa (see-sa) —ten, 10; two hand hands, with palms together

Snaugbmen (Snauw-g-men) —family, clan name

Snomoch (Sno-moch) —son of Sogora and Deiyagaris

Sogora (So-go-ra) —first ancestor of the Saiba clan

Sougb (So-gb) —The People, a tribal group of people in Papua, Indonesia

sorama (sor-am-a) — fifteen; two hands, plus grasp one foot

Sud hom —twenty; one person; two hands and two feet

Sud hom sisa edaysu (sud hom see-sa e-day-soo) -thirty, 30; one person, plus two hands

Sud hom; dara mairesi, dara mebes, dara mums, dara mops, dara marij; or
   one person; plus, eyes, ears, nose holes, lips and breasts

Sud hwai —forty, 40; two people

Sud hwai sisa edaysu —fifty, 50; two people, plus two hands

Sud homoy (sud ho-moy) —sixty, 60; three people

Sud sergem (ser-gem) —one hundred; five people

Sunggwadis (Soong-gwa-dis) —village up valley from Sururay village

Sururay (Soo-roo-ray) —village by Anggi Lake

Suwu (Soo-woo) —snake's name

T

Testega (tes-te-ga) —village by the lake

Tuan (too-an) —lord, Colonial term of respect

tuan-ged (too-an-ged) -most common, red beads

tu medgomori (med-go-mor-ee) —skeleton frame

tu mayj (too may-j) -temporary hut

tu menau (too me-now) —new house

tu moguray (too mog-u-rei) —little house, birthing hut

tu mohon (too mo-hon) —old house

U

Ubas (oo-bas) —uncle to Desingmei, killed by soldiers in World War 2

uf (oof) — from a certain palm leaf, used for roofing

Ugdaren (Oog-da-ren) —man's name

Unyai (Oon-yai) —place where suspected water creature lives

Ugwamonggamod (Oo-gwa-mong-ga-mod) —name of a mountain

W

Wausugb (Wow-soogb) Falls   —waterfalls near Sihu in district of Nenay village

Appendix I. Geneologies

We Sougb people did not have our voice written down until 1965 when the missionaries came into our land. Everything we heard about our history was passed down to us from the voices of our grandfathers, grandmothers and also our parents. Below is a list of the generations of our clans. The first Sougb family started with a man named Igba (Eeg-ba). Grandfather Yonaden remembered all the Ahoren (A-ho-ren) clan names, which came down as sons and daughters of Igba. Father Harun listed all of the Inden (In-den) generations. Old Grandfather Ee-jom-me-di-go recited the ancestors of the Inyomusi (Een-yo-mu-si) clan. One generation is about thirty years long. I am glad that all the families are written down in this book and the names will never be forgotten. Our family names are important to us because they prove our identity as a People. —Dessy

Ancestors Remembered
Grandfathers of the Sougb People
Clans: Ahoren, Inden, Saiba, Douansiba, Mandachan, Inden and Inyomus

Igba's female ancestor: Douansiba
> Villages of Testega, Trigdaga, Taigeh,
>> Tombrog, Bintuni, Duhugbeiya, Duhwigba

Igba's ancestors of the Bohon (Nenay) dialect:
> Villages of Misbairo, Sisgera, Korob, IsimMedibo, DibesMedibo

Igba's other ancestors: found in other areas
> Villages of Hugomod, Disiaga, Bomi, Adboma, Aroba

Ahoren Family Generations: from Yonaden Ahoren, Kofo Village

> **Ahoren** - his father Sira
> +
> **Sira -** his father Bachi
> +
> **Bachi -** his father Dougwa
> +
> **Dougwa** - his father Inden
>
> **Inden** - his father Isiya
> +
> **Isiya** - his father Dougwen
> +

Dougwen - his father Igba
   +
Igba

Sira had seven sons:
   Ahoren (village of Sururay)
      +
   Saiba (village of Sururay)
      +
   Lougb (village of Bamaha-Testega)
      +
   Howan (village of Suapen)
      +
   Merero (village of Drologo)
      +
   Hugbay (village of Sneremer)
      +
   Inya (village of Sisgemaymetaha)

Grandfather Yonaden Ahoren's Family Ancestors:

Ahoren   +   **Doubud (wife)**
(villages of Anaymes,   (village of Hosma)
Adboma, Derugwera, Chingga)

Their children:
- **-Amongga**
- **-Duhugwayj** +   Sons: **Mauduhu**
- **-Ihwayj**   **+**
- **-Srora**   **Maij**
-          **+**   **+**
- **4 daughters**   **Adem**
-   **+**
-   **Merehi**
-   **+**
-             **Grandfather-Pastor Yonaden** (Kofo)

Inden Generations from Igba

Father-Pastor Harun Inden, Disi & Nenay Villages

Name	Village	Children
Igba	(Duhwigba/Bintuni)	Isiya, **Douansiba**, Dougben Darij Ahway
+		
Isiya	(Duhwigba/Bintuni)	
+		
Inden	(Isim-Medibo)	many sons: **Ahoren, Inyomusi**, etc.
+		
Mers	(Gorob)	
+		
***Ugwareij**	(Gorob)	Siremes, Sbogo, Mayn, Sa, Daugduhu, Dau
+		
Siremes	(Disi)	
+		
Mahamai	(Disi)	
+		
girl **Debro**	(Disi)	

+ husband = **Augouji Saiba** (Sunggwadis)
  +

Horai	(Disi)	
+ wife **Daydara**	(Duhugbaya)	**Harun**, Dochebin, Dorkas, Dosum
+ wife Biag		Pontrikus, Iskariod Douro

+

Harun Inden (Disi-Nenay)

+ wife **Aksemina**	+	Yorpinche, Susan, Nita

Inden Grandfathers: Harun Inden, Nenay

Ugwareij (Gorob) other children:

- **Siremes** the firstborn, eldest son

- **Sbogo** (Gorob)   son Ijou + son Sagwihi
son Ibeij + son Udarouh
(DibesMedibo/Misbairo)

- **Daugduhu**   married **Sayori**

- **Mayn**   (Gorob)   son Lougdia + son Iborhoy
(DibesMedibo)

- **Dau** (Kofo)   +   wife **Duhuhwayj**, son Merehi,
his son **Yonaden,**
Yonaden's grandfather **Ahoren**

Inyomusi Family Tree

Grandfather Ijom-medigo Inyomusi of Disihu (Iray) Village

Ijommedigo (Anuk)   wife Dochabero Ahoren (Kachu's sister)
   +
Bauh (Anuk)   wife Gowi family, died
wife Darayj from the Ijom (Hatam)
   +
Inyomus (Hosma)   wife Diara (Titaho)
   +
Maynyoho (Hosma, Dirirbo)
   +
Meb (Loinya, from Nenay dialect, and Inohumay of the Sougb dialect,
places near IsimMedibo)

***These family names were collected and written down in 1998 by Barbara Lunow.
Before that time, all the names were memorized by appointed eldest sons, fathers
and grandfathers, who passed them down to younger generations for their
remembrance.*

Appendix II. Dowry System and Bride Price

My people have a payment system, called dowry, for marriages and also for other events in our culture like: fights between villages, stealing, sexual affairs and accusations of using black magic. Since we do not have money, we use certain goods in place of it. The things that we use for payments and trading things are: pigs, strings of glass beads, carved shell armbands and head pieces, bolts of cloth, and a special woven cloth, called Kain Timor. The woven pieces are very old and we can't get them anymore. The stores in town now have cheaper fabric that we buy. The bolts are not of great value in dowry payments.

The original beads and cloth were traded long ago when strangers came in sailing ships to the coastal village settlements. Boats from the island of Timor brought pieces of woven cloth that were about the size of a blanket. It was woven on a loom in dark blue colors with patterns of red and white. These pieces are the oldest and most valuable of our cloth; some are 250-300 years old according to the generations.

—Dessy

Appendix III. Dowry Beads
Types of beads: no longer available, all are glass beads and generations old

leemaga = light yellow, no longer seen

leemeij = darker yellow, sharp edging, no longer seen

leeampoum = large, blue, sharp edge, from Chinese traders, or foreigners from the island of Ternate, Indonesia, very old and valuable

sariou = rare pearls, or white beads with cloisonné design, from Chinese traders, valuable

leemaga merij = common, smaller, light yellow, old

chugwemera = faded red, round, large, from early Dutch traders

leebogo = rare, darker blue, small and round, early Dutch

leemogo gogoufu = common, white beads, early Dutch, fewer

mem prau = cheap, red and yellow beads, from a certain Dutch store on the coast

tuan-ged = most common, red beads